Raven's Children

Raven's Children

WORD SKETCHES
OF
THE LAND
AND
NATIVE ARCTIC PEOPLES
OF

Alaska

BY
Jacques L. Condor
Maka Tai Meh

iUniverse, Inc.
New York Lincoln Shanghai

Raven's Children
WORD SKETCHES OF THE LAND AND NATIVE ARCTIC PEOPLES
OF Alaska

iUniverse, Inc.

For information address:
iUniverse
2021 Pine Lake Road, Suite 100
Lincoln, NE 68512
www.iuniverse.com

ISBN: 0-595-28867-7 (Pbk)
ISBN: 0-595-74928-3 (Cloth)

Printed in the United States of America

Raven's Children

IS FOR

Diana and Michelle

The two Ladies in my life
who love
ALASKA
As much as
I do

Preface

The first time visitor making a trip to Alaska soon finds that all the superlatives and over-the-top adjectives used to describe *The Great Land* are true. Up here the mountains *are* higher, the land area *so* vast, the changing scenery *more* spectacular than almost any other place on earth, and the people...all of Alaska's people...more daring, more adventurous and more enterprising than most.

The people who come to Alaska are the dreamer types, the majority are running to fulfil a dream or running from a dream gone sour. Those who choose to stay are rewarded in ways they may not have imagined. The indigenous peoples of Alaska who came to this immense peninsula over forty thousand years ago must have been dreamers; perhaps dreaming of a better life in a new world. This first peoples must have felt the same awe, experienced the same exhilaration and sensed the rewards to be had just as the current crop of contemporary visitors and inhabitants do.

The Aleut of the Islands, the Athabascan of the interior, the Totem People of the Southeast and the Yupik and Inupiat of the Tundra, the last two lumped together as "*Eskimo*", stayed on and developed some of the most advanced cultures on the North American continent. I refer to the Tlingits, Haida and Tsimshian. The Athabascan inherited the wooded areas, the lakes and rivers and built a arresting culture that has endured. The sea-faring Aleut made the ocean and its bounty their own and survived a century of maltreatment and slavery at the hands of the Russian fur traders. But is the people of the high Arctic, the ones labeled *Eskimo,* who won my respect and my heart from the first time I journeyed to their lands.

Nowhere on earth are the conditions so harsh; the land so inhospitable. No where else is nature so determined to work against man. And yet these remarkably adaptive people have made the bleak treeless Arctic their home and thrived; surviving into the twenty-first century and maintaining an admirable and ancient culture while accepting and integrating the new and dominant ways. In this land of unimaginable cold, half-year darkness survival of a race seemed unlikely...but survive they did!

I first encountered the Yupik and Inupiat peoples in 1939 when I came to live in Nome with a paternal aunt who had been a pioneer in what was then a frost-heave-tilted, weather-mutilated colourless little town on the grey Bering Sea.

Each summer the people from King Island came across the water to make camp on the beach front at Nome. I discovered them and they acknowledged me (as an outsider) but still invited me to visit with them as often as I liked. The great and venerable chief Olarana welcomed the ten year old I was then to his camp. I watched and learned; words, customs and proper behavior. These first lessons served me well later when I lived among the Yupik of Saint Lawrence Island and then among other groups including Inupiat people.

Many thousands of miles and more than sixty years later I continued to be fascinated and surprised by the *Eskimo* people whom I admire and honor. I have visited major *Eskimo* settlements and villages across Alaska and Canada. I spent time with the Denendeh of the northern forest and the Kutchin of the Arctic Circle region.

My respect for these dwellers on the edge of nowhere continues to increase the more I learn of their culture and history. This respect for them needed expression. So I have gone back to my old journals and other sources to create these '*Word Sketches*' to honor these incredible people. (I hesitate to call these writings '*poetry*' but perhaps that's what they are.) Among the *Eskimo* I have never learned a word for '*poetry*' but an editor of *Eskimo* works, Edmund Carpenter, uses the word '*Anernerk*'. This is a difficult word with many meanings, among them:' *breath*' and '*spirit*'.

I would like to hope that these efforts to portray these dwellers in the Land-of-Long-Shadows are infused with the *breath and spirit* of their culture and lives today as well as in other times and other places.

Jacques L. Condor

Maka Tai Meh

Sun City, Arizona 2003

Acknowledgments and Credits

These *word sketches* about the indigenous peoples of the Arctic Rim are as original as my memories and journals can make them be. Songs and chants heard forty years ago have bubbled to the surface and I have made them my own…at least the interpretations are my own work Some of these *word-sketches* are based on translations from Danish, French, German, Russian and Yupik or Inupiat works and sources. I would like to thank my friends, multi-lingual persons all, who have, over the years, helped me personally or indirectly through their works with languages I do not speak. My thanks to Anne Marie Collins, Frank Mercer, Evangeline Hahn, Hulda Svenson, Dieter and Johanna Carlson, Ollie Palmer, Jenny Martin, Emma Willoaugh, Ticasuk/ Emily Ivanoff Brown, Betty Phelps-Scott, Arthur Theibert, O.M.I., Reverend John Hinz, Steven A. Jacobson and Vera Uqiitlek Oovi Kaneshiro.

My thanks to Writers of the Alaskan scene and to the people who have been sources for many of the songs and chants in this book. I particulary want to acknowledge the inspiration of Lael Morgan's work and her marvelous writings over the years. The books of Ticasuk, Emily Ivanoff Brown, Richard K. Nelson, Louise Gore, Wally Heibert, Sally Carrighar, James Houston, Claire Fejes, Jim Huntington and Arthur Hansin Eide, all who have taught me so much more about the Great Land and inspired me to write. I am also indebted to Alaska Magazine, Alaska Native Magazine, National Geographic Magazine and the Time Life Books on Alaska and the Canadian North. Details I missed when I lived among the people of the north were waiting to be discovered in the pages of these magazines.

I did not intend to create a bibliography for this small book, in reality, I couldn't. A bibliography on the books about Alaska and the Arctic regions of Canada, Greenland and Siberia I have collected and read over the past sixty years would require more pages and be a much bigger book than the one you hold in your hands. I will, however, append a List of the books on the subjects; books that I have enjoyed most and recommend.

JLC/MTM

Contents

A CHILD'S SONG: KUSKOKWIM DELTA, ALASKA 1939

Now sing a song of Summer!
The time when geese can't fly.

Now, beat the round skin drum, our happiness sing out and loudly stomp your feet.

Now sing a song of summer!
Sister Sun dances high.

Now, beat the round skin drum, our happiness sing out and loudly stomp your feet.

Now sing a song of summer!
Green grass and nests of eggs.

Now, beat the round skin drum, our happiness sing out and loudly stomp your feet.

Now sing a song of summer!
Young things on wobbly legs.

Now, beat the round skin drum, our happiness sing out and loudly stomp your feet.

Now sing a song of summer!
Her time has come at last.

Now, beat the round skin drum, our happiness sing out and loudly stomp your feet.

Sing of life and summer days
For both can never last!

Sing of life and summer days
For both can never last!

Sing of life and summer days
For both can never last!

We saw the caribou calf
drop from his mother's warmth
and
in his natal pouch
struggle.
Twitch
on frost-crisped ground.

We saw him free.
Breathing.
Watched him waver stand
then fall
to stand again.

Saw his wide-eyed fear.
Caused by what?
The new unknown?
Cold world encountered?
or perhaps
it was his mother's
terror.

Frantic bleating.
She sensed circling wolves
Her fear
caused baby eyes to roll white.
Mother ran, not far.
And
circled back.
Back through the ring of wolves.

We saw him struggle.
Trying
his stick-legs.
Long, wide hoofed.
Clumsy.
He tried to trot
following his mother's bleats
but fell.

And then,
the wolves
Cut between cow and calf
Teeth bared
Gnashing and crippling.
Ripping.
Taking life.
killing the mute thing that was,
just before, new life
New life of hope
Hope, future promise for his kind
Never fulfilled.

True life.
An observation.

We saw the pup seal, cream-white
On the flow at the breathing hole
Scratched through
thickest ice
by diligent mother.
Weak Arctic sun
circled low.
The pup's shadow
Long, purple, reflected
lengthened
across the ice hummocks

Nanook.
Great white mass of death.
Long-limbed plunderer
Of the Ice plains.
Death bear
sensed the shadow on the ice.
Heard the faintest
clicking sound
of pup seal's scratching claws

The harp-seal mother
heard same faint sound
and
rose from beneath the ice
called to heed
pups nursing need.
Great bear waited.

Movements halted.
He froze.
His killing paw aloft and ready.

One blow.
The seal mother ripped
From her breathing hole.
Pup,
First noticed,
Last to die
was cruelly taken.
His crumpled body, wasted.
Only baby blubber
Fat, buttery yellow-white, life sustaining
was eaten.

True life
An observation.

We saw the truth of life
that day.
Saw the plan of whom?
What scheme of things demanded
young things
Be taken
Before life was lived
but moments?

Cruel un-feeling scheme,
It seems.

Pain-bringing
to those who witness young things gone
in an instant.
Cruel mind-searing memories
with me still.
And yet,
I remember
hard learned
wise words of my Yupik companion.

"We see the young
of animal brothers taken.
Swift is death.
Common here and constant.
So it is
we value, even more,
the children who come to us.
We cannot know
What unseen pursuer
waits to take them
from us,
So we love and guard our children well."

True life.
An observation.

DOG CHILDREN OF THE WOLF: EKLUTNA VILLAGE, ALASKA 1975

From the scrub spruce forest
From the distant mountains foot,
A wolf howls.
Calls to the night moon
Rising over Knik Arm of the inlet.
A wolf howls.
The moon listens.
The wolf howls and
All the dogs in our village
Rise from their curled seep
And point their muzzles to the sky.
This night,
They sing the night songs
To the moon
With their wolf father,
Waking us all.
Tomorrow,
When the sun's light frees us
From the dark,
The night singers,
The wolf's dog-children
The howlers
Will be dogs again.
Wagging their tails and
Begging food.
Their night song forgotten.

NORTHERN LIGHTS: KOTZEBUE, ALASKA, 1953

Look!
The colours dance across the frozen sky!
Flashing high in the winter night.
Look!
The colours wave and dip, curl and rise.
Look!
The spirits of our people
Are playing a game.
The spirits of our people
Are leaping, running, playing ball.
The spirit ones play a game of kickball
With a walrus head
Thrown around
Up there in the sky.
The spirits run, kick
And leap
Playing a game.
And lighting up the winter sky.

CARIBOU HUNTER: ANIKTOOVIK PASS, ALASKA 1959

Now, I dream you, caribou.
I hear the clicking rhythm of your hooves
And the sound is music to my ears.
If I dream you will you come?

Now I see you, caribou.
Your antlers glistening shine pleases my eye.
Your silhouette against the morning sky
Quickens the drum of my heart.

Now I want you, caribou.
Your flesh is sweet and good for our feasting.
Your skin warm and thick for making our boots.
Your bones and antlers I use.

Now I hunt you, caribou
I follow you running so fast down wind.
How swift, how fleet your slim legs so graceful
Moving tireless as you flee.

Now I track you, caribou.
You skim the frozen ground, gliding away.
My bullets cannot find you in the brush.
You hide behind willow scrub.

Now I loose you, caribou.
Circling hidden wolves followed on your trail.
You scent them and turn back to run toward me.
Wolf-fright drives you to your death.

Now I take you, caribou!

REINCARNATION: POINT HOPE ALASKA, 1837

My old grandfather, Panniaq
died three days ago.
My heart is full of sadness.
I miss the old one.
Today my mother hums to herself.
She is no longer sad.
Yesterday my mother's sister
birthed a baby boy.
My mother is joyful.
She says Grandfather has returned to us.
The new baby they called, Panniaq.
I went with my mother
to see my infant grandfather.
The baby does have the old one's eyes
but my grandfather, Panniaq,
never made such a noise
when he was hungry.

A MARRIAGE ARRANGED: KIVALINA, ALASKA 1880

Do not fret so, my pretty daughter.
The man you marry is kind.
I have chosen him for you
From among the others.
Your mother approves of my choice.
It is done
And arranged
With his family
All will be well in time.

Do not weep so, my favored daughter.
The man you marry is good.
I have chosen you a much skilled hunter.
Our dwelling will never lack meat.
It is done
And arranged
With his family, my daughter
Now pull back your parka hood.

Do not frown so, my little daughter.
The man you marry looks good.
I have chosen him just for you.
I did this because I love you
My only daughter,
The best you deserve and I found him.
Be happy with your husband
Who comes now
And
Offer marriage feast gifts of food.

MAKE PRAYERS TO THE RAVEN:
DENENDEH, NORTHWEST TERRITORIES, 1957

Make prayers to the Raven,
All who live in the great north woods.
Oh, Dene brotherhood.

Make prayers to the Raven,
Give thanks for blessings and for good.
Oh, Dene brotherhood.

Make prayers to the Raven,
His power finds and brings us food.
Oh, Dene brotherhood.

Make prayers to the Raven,
All who live in the great north wood.
Oh, Dene brotherhood.

Make prayers to the Raven,
Who guides us as he said he would.
Oh, Dene Brotherhood.

Make prayers to the Raven,
Greet his relations as you should.
Oh, Dene brotherhood.

Make prayers to the Raven,
So his power is understood.
Oh, Dene brotherhood.

Make prayers to the Raven,
For protection in this wild wood.
Make prayers to the Raven,
Slavey, Dog-Rib, Hare, and Gwich'in,
Mountain, Bear Lake, Chipewyan,
Oh, Dene brotherhood,
Denendeh!
Land of Grandfather Raven.

THE WINDS: UTQIAGVIK, ALASKA 1553

The winds blow.
The winds change.
The winds change
the landscape,
the people,
our lives
The winds change the world we know.
The winds scour our souls
And
howling,
blow unknown Inupiat memories
through the empty chambers of our hollow hearts.

SOUTH WINDS

Her husband is a great hunter.
He feeds his family
and those in need.
He stalks the wily oogruk
and
fat walrus on the ice flows streaming north
before the south winds.

He does not return,
Her husband.
On the shore, alone, far from the villagers,
she wails her sorrow
into
the hissing south winds.
The slushing sounds,
grinding ice sounds of
shifting ice carry her widow-cries far out to sea.
As they, these
scudding sudden warm south winds
carried
her hunter husband to his
death in the arms
of Sila beneath the waves.

EAST WINDS

A full cycle of the moon
has passed since he died, her husband.
She is a young woman still.
Two men have paid court to her
but
she will not admit them to
hearth or heart.
She lives a widow's life in a new sod house
Isolated,
east of the village on the bluff above the sea.
She built a home.
For her drowned husbands children,
for her young sister
their old mother.
The east winds pushed driftwood,
polished silver-grey to the foot of the bluff.
The east winds told her to
To build here.
The east winds provided.

WEST WINDS

West winds came with the winter.
The time of long darkness
had come.
The widow with
her family made preparations.
The storm would come soon and last,
perhaps,
for half a moon.
The widow trimmed her lamps.
Her small son checked the dogs.
The sister brought food into the sod house
from storage racks.
The old mother built a fire to
melt snow for drinking
prepare meals in advance.
Preparations complete, the family
Settled down to wait out the storm.

In the night
the long night,
the storm expanded
The west winds screamed
labored to drive the sea ice to shore
then
shrieked among the slabs of ice
piled high against the bluff.
Ice, tossed chunks of ice flew with the west wind
across the bluff toward the village.
The lone house on the bluff,
Half-buried in the earth for warmth
and safety, creaked,
shuddered against the strength of the winds.
In the sod house
the family tossed and turned.
Fear slept within the house as well.
The widow spoke
To her children,
softly, forcing calm into her words.
The house is intact.
We have nothing to fear.
We have made preparations.

CHANGING WINDS

The family
had weathered past storms.
But then there had been a man in the home.
His presence brought a sense of
of strength against a storm.
Alone now,
the widow did as she had been taught.
To dispel fear
She sang songs
from her sleeping place.
Songs of comfort and caring.
Songs to bring quiet to fear-steeped hearts.
The storm howled
She sang.

Suddenly,
without a sign or warning, huge chunks of ice,
the dreaded *ivu* came.
Tongues,
giant tongues of ice
jumbled against the shore, rose high.
Burst free.
Slab-like and rising immense
Above the rim of the bluff.
Then
Pushed from below by the changing winds
roared up and over the bluff.
The ice surge sent the giant slabs of ice
Up, over and then
down.
Down on the tiny house
nestled on the bluff.
The roof bent.
Collapsed.
Under the *ivu's* onslaught nothing,
nothing
could stand.
Not the house
Not the family within, nothing.
The house crashed inward and down.
Crushing everything.
Flesh and furs
Preparations and lives gone.
Obliterated under ice.
Under the *ivu*
Quickly and then quietly
death
came with the *ivu*.
The changing winds silenced themselves.
Shuffled away across the pack ice.
Silence.
Nothing more.

NORTH WINDS

Morning.
Morning darkness
The stubborn winds
the howling winds were gone.
Villagers awoke
Crawled the passage ways of their homes
to smell
north winds and new snow.
North wind brought hushed quiet
and
fresh snow.
There was much visiting from home to home.
Checking.
Inquiring if all was well.
Chattering about the crashing sounds
grinding sounds of ice in the night.
When some went to the place.
East of the village.
On the bluff.
Where the widow lived.
They saw only ice.
Slabs of ice.
Towers of shore ice.
Tongues of ice thrust up and over the bluff
Where the house had been
There was only ice.
No sound, no barking dogs
No scent of cooking fire smoke.
People shook their heads.
Muttered about *ivu* and death
People turned away.
Left the bluff and did not look back.
The north winds brought
snow.
All through the dark day, snow.
Quickly and quietly as death
The snow covered
the white shroud of ice congealing,
over the cold and lifeless house.
The whiteness erased the tragedy
And
the memory of the widow
and her family.

THE WINDS OF TIME

Generations come.
Generations go.
Shuffling footsteps
Across boggy tundra, winter ice, spring snow.
Four hundred or more years
Shuffle by,
Toe-in-Inupiat shuffling.
The land is called Alaska.
Utquiagvik becomes Barrow,
Kabloonaq approach the land.
Russians come, Russians go.
Americans come.
They do not go.
Ships and whalers, oil lamps and sails.
Sleek planes
Will Rogers and Wiley Post.
Oil and pipelines
And with them,
Archeologists searchers for our Inupiat past.
Through them
The memory of the widow
And her family
Lives again.
The winds of time exposed their frozen forms.
The archeologists
pried them from their frozen tomb,
the little house on the bluff.
Disinterred, they were studied.
Analyzed.
Carbon dated and
reburied.
An Inupiat graveyard.
with Christian songs.
Hymns,
their ancient spirit-souls could not understand.
The winds of time bring
Many things. changes.
That which is progress
And memories.

THE WINDS

The winds blow.
The winds change.
The winds change the
the landscape.
the people,
our lives.
The winds change the world we know.
The winds scour our souls
and
howling,
blow unknown Inupiat memories
through the empty chambers of our hollow hearts.

THERE IS A MASK-MAKER IN OUR VILLAGE: ANAKTUVIK PASS 1955

There is a mask-maker in our village.
He is called
Akkaq.
He is my father's half-brother
and therefore,
my Uncle.
He is old.
His face is lined and
his eyes disappear into his high and bony cheeks
when he laughs.
Which is often.
My old Uncle Akkaq makes masks
of shaved caribou skins.
My father sells them.
To the tourist shops
in Anchorage.
The money my father gets
from these masks
buy us many good things.
Sugar.
Flour.
Chocolate and best of all,
tea.
When tourists come
flying in
to visit our village
my old uncle sells the masks to them.
They stoop coming in
the small door of our house
where he works
making the masks.
Tourist eyes are big with surprise
when they see how we live.
They wrinkle their noses
and try
To pretend they
Do not smell the raw caribou hides
or my Uncle's glue pot
stinking of boiled caribou hooves and bones.

Their white voices
ask many questions of my Uncle.
They haggle.
Try to bargain down the prices
my father sets.
My father is stubborn.
He keeps the prices where he wants them to be.
My old Uncle Akkaq laughs
And mutters insults at the bargaining tourists.
He smiles and they smile back.
Not knowing he has called them *tiglikte,* thieves.
They always buy.
for my Uncle's masks are marvels
Each one made
from a new mold he carves.
Over each new mold he presses
wet caribou hides.
Glues a fur ruff about the face
and lets them dry
before
Pulling them from the wooden molds.
Once a tourist asked
why he made a new mold for each face.
Told my Uncle
try the white man's mass production.
My Uncle laughed
And replied
in English the tourist did not expect
It is told.
When great Creator-Spirit
first made man he made each man's face different
so we could recognize one another.
Broke the mold after each one.
It is the Creator-Spirit
Who gives
my hands this talent to make faces.
Can I do less
Than follow Creators example?
The tourist gaped,
his mouth a round hole in his face
before he closed it.
Embarrassed, he coughed
and bought three masks from my father.

HAIKU FOR THE NEW WORLD

ADVICE TO A DAUGHTER: YUPIK VILLAGE, ALASKA 1953

Listen to your heart
Our drum beats truth in the songs
Others may not dance.

OLARANA: KING ISLAND ALASKA, 1951

Piebald face, fur ruff
Long arms beating wooden drum
Wolf dancers spring out!

INUPIAT HUNTER'S SONG: NORTHWEST ALASKA 1952

Good fortune!
Today I have taken the mighty seal Oogruk,
Great bearded seal
Mountain of fat and blubber,
Meat for many families,
Another skin for a new Umiak.

Good fortune!
Today I give honor to the mighty Oogruk,
Great bearded seal.
Give honor and pay respect
Send his soul back to his realm
Let him depart without anger or need.

Good fortune!
Today I give him this fresh snow water to drink.
Great bearded seal.
You will not know thirst again.
Now the water comforts you.
Your soul is free. Depart in peace this day.

Good fortune!
Today I have treated you well, my friend, Oogruk.
Great bearded seal.
And your skin was not defiled
By blood of land animal.
Therefore, speak well of me in your dark realm.

Good fortune!
Today I will be a hunter long remembered.
Great bearded seal.
Speak now to the other seals
Tell them to give me their bodies
So my village will survive cruel winter.
Assure them I will return their souls.

HAIKU FOR A DEAD SEAL'S SOUL: POINT HOPE, ALASKA 1947

Bear me no grudge, seal.
Fresh water wets your black nose.
Liberated soul.

I am Innuit.
A man who took your body
Set free, soul, leave us

Depart now, free soul
Speak to waiting souls I hunt.
Go now soul of seal.

In your wide mouth, seal
I have spit fresh melt water
Go, soul, to your realm.

Leave us, depart now
Inform your kin in the sea
How honored you were.

Innuit hands kill
Liberating your seal-soul
Thank you for your gifts.

Depart, go, depart
Tell others who swim below
Honor awaits them here

THE DEATH OF A WHALING CAPTAIN: POINT HOPE, ALASKA 1890

This man Tarraq,
Has seen more than eighty years.
He has taken fifty whales in his time.
He was,
In his youth, our strongest man.
Stout of body
Full of chest
Keen of eye.
No passing whale could escape his sweeping glance.
At the whale feasts he was honored,
Esteemed by all the village.
The people sang songs of him
And danced
The story of his many whale-hunts.
The songs
Told of the way he guided us
Between danger
Drifting flows that might have taken our umiak.
The songs
Told of how he knew where the whale would erupt
From the sea depths.
Now Tarraq is gone.
Four days have passed since he sat in the captain's place
In our umiaks
He led our whale hunt
But he did not see the drifting floes
Floes
That could slice the skin boat's sides
Tarraq did not see the great whale that surfaced to our side.
His old eyes
Burned and worn by glare
By years of searching
Did not help us.
Our umiaks returned with no whale in tow.
On the third day of our return
He filled his trousers
His parka and boots with pebbles
And waded into the sea.
We could not stop him.
This death was his wish, his right.

WHITE WHALES: CAPE WALES, ALASKA 1970

The fat white whales are here!
Massed close they blow
In the inlet.
They came with the tide
They are stranded
See them watch us!
The beluga are here!

Hurry! Run! Shout the news!
Come see the whales!
They play they feed.
We cannot take them!
Government men
Down in Juneau
Decreed laws against us

Whales do not know such laws.
They think we kill.
That hunters come
To seal the inlet.
Encircle them
Herd them, drive them
With sharp harpoon waiting.

See them splash and writhe now.
Their eyes hold fear
Their flukes tremble
See how they watch us.
We watch them back.
We cannot kill.
We will send them out soon.

The fat white whales are here!
Massed close they blow
In the inlet.
They go with the tide.
To open sea
To swim away.
They leave us on the shore.

The beluga are gone!
The tide took them.
Bore them to safety
And Juneau laws.
Protected them from our lances

Quiet, we stand on shore
Some of the women sob
The men curse
Much meat, many skins
For lines, boot soles
Swim away from our shore.

Never mind, it is done.
Juneau men say
We send supplies.
The boat will come.
Planes will circle, land.
Supplies cost much
Whales are free for taking.
Juneau men don't know this.

THE WAY IT IS HERE: KIVALINA, ALASKA 1900

The moon is strongest
He has defeated the sun.
She was too weak to stand the coming cold anyway.
She has fled far away
To where there are trees,
Or so I am told, for I have never seen a living tree
Only their bleached white driftwood bodies
clogging the sand-spit's shore.
The night is long
Longer than you can imagine.
Darkness is our constant companion in this village now.
Seal oil in the lamps cannot hold it always at bay.
Darkness wins when the oil is gone.
The winds howl and shake our home
As the white bear shakes the seal.
Hunger waits, prowls at the edges of our village
Ready to hurry in when the food caches are empty.
Sickness follows hunger, always.
Some evil spirits stalk through our village unseen
And bring sickness
We can sing.
We can consult the angakoks with their charms and powers
But that is all we can do.
Those angakoks, those shaman-magicians
They cannot push back the darkness
Or the cold
They cannot call back the weak sun
If she is too timid to answer their summons
And their charms and drummed spells
Cannot drive out the hunger
And the sickness.
That's the way it is here.
We have grown accustomed to the long night
The cold
The hunger
The sickness
The deaths.
We are only men.

LOVE CHARMS: NOATAK, ALASKA 1920

She is so pleasant to look at
So pretty to my eyes.
Her face is round and plump.
And thick in the middle.
She will make a good wife.
Tireless and strong.
Her teeth are white her jaws are strong
She will chew many hides.
Her fingers are nimble
Her eyes are bright.
She will sew me fine clothes.
Her thighs are strong
I can lie between them
and make children with her.
I need this woman to wife
But she does not notice me.
I will go to the angakok for a love charm.

I bought a love charm
From the angakok-magician.
I paid with a kayak and a promise
Of fresh meat through one moon's changing.
That charm cost me dear
But the angakok,
He guaranteed its power.
I placed the charm inside the passageway
of her house
Under a flat stone
Where the dogs could not get it.
I waited four days.
When I passed her on the trail to the river
She did not look at me.
I will wait four more days.

Four days have passed.
I will go near her house and watch her.
See there! She comes out of the passageway.
She does not look at me.
Even though I see my love charm
In her fingers.
She holds it like a rotted lemming found under a bed roll.
She keeps it far away from her body
Holding it with arm stiff.
The charm will work now!
I think and wait for her
To notice me
And
Smile and come toward me
But
She only shakes the leather bundle of my charm
To see if it makes a sound.
She puts it to her nose and sniffs
She makes a face of disgust
Then
Rips open the love charm with her ulu-knife
And lets the contents fall
To the ground.
Her dog sniffs at the bones and dried things on the ground
And then
Snaps them up, greedily.
My breath catches in my throat.
I think of the price the angakok demanded
I want to shout
"Look at me, Love me! Live with me!"
But
I do not
She does not even notice me
Standing there.
She only pats the rump of her dog
And goes back into her house.
I go up and kick her dog.

WINTER SOLSTICE: NOME, ALASKA, 1954

Full moon.
White orb.
hangs on the Arctic night
like
bleached skin-drum.
Silver light
cold moon-fire
pale
incandescent, constant
illuminates
the landscape.
Mounds
and more mounds of whiteness
like
rolling waves frozen,
immobile
stretch toward
distant low mountains.
Wraiths of snow.
Dry pellets
sand-like,
writhe white ghost-trails up
and
around snow hummocks.
Hissing,
grains of snow
Hissing
with raspy breath.
Puffs of frigid air
Scatter them in the night.
The traveler
approaches the mounded village.
Dry snow
sweeps in
to hide his footstep traces.
From the mounds
tethered sled dogs burst free
at his approach.
Erupt from
snow bed-tombs
and howl as he passes

TO DANCE FOR THE ELDERS: YUPIK, KWETHLUK, ALASKA, 1970

Tonight
in the Kashim
for the elders and my family
for all the assembled people of my village,
I will dance.
My 'First Dance' it is called.
First Dance.
to show
I am ready to enter the life of my people.
I will be recognized as a person
I have come or age
I am responsible
as one of the people.

Tonight
I will hear
the beating thunder
of the walrus hide drums.
I will dance
to their booming beating.
I will wear
a new cotton parka my mother has made.
New mukluks
and
a head-dress of beads and fur.
Long strands of wolverine plumes on my head-dress
will sway
keeping time to the drum.
In my moving hands
I will hold
finger fans of caribou hair.
Breath feathers
from the snowy owl
will quiver on the fan tips as if alive
and dancing, too.

Tonight
I will dance.
My first dance.
I will dance a story for the elders.
For
my family and the assembled people.
Beneath my feet,
my father
will place a perfect seal skin
for me
to stand on when I dance.
It will be an honor I will never know again.
The drummers
will chant a song for my story-dance.
I will sway and make my body
obey.
Obey the pounding rhythms of the drums.
Tonight
I will be brave before the elders; all the people.
I will dance my best.
I will
accept this honor
and
become a grown-up person.
But now,
as I prepare
for this dance, my 'First Dance'
I am still a little girl
and
I am afraid.

LITTLE GRANDMOTHER: SAINT MARY'S MISSION, ALASKA 1919

In the month when the geese cannot fly,
My old Grandmother Ekaterina left us.
She went to dance with the ancestors
In the lights of the northern sky.

Four days after her funeral in the church
After we marked her grave in the churchyard,
My cousin Sophia gave birth to a baby girl.
In the middle of our grief, happiness came.

My mother whispered to me and told me
My grandmother had returned to us
This new baby girl of my cousin was proof.
She was named at once and called Ekaterina.

The mission priest did not whisper.
He spoke loud words against my mother.
Said she was heretic and followed old ways.
Denounced the reincarnation of my grandmother.

I listened to the priest but shut my heart's ears.
I grieved long for my lost grandmother
Made no visit to the new baby or cousin Sophia.

Three changes of the moon later I made a visit.
My mother held the baby on her knee
When the baby reached out her arms to me,
Tilted her baby head just so and smiled,
I knew!

The mission priest comes from another place
Knows only the things of another world.
His faraway world not ours here
He is not one of the people and our ways
Now, in spite of him,
I call my cousin Sophia's baby 'Little grandmother'.
That is her name in our village.

Timertik, big walrus is wise.
He keeps his distance from the scent of man.
Knows that man eats his flesh
Takes his ivory tusks.

Timertik, big walrus is lazy.
Will not swim when he can float
Knows fresh water ice will break
Salt water ice is tough.

Timertik, big walrus is curious.
Will turn to face man's whistled call.
Knows something strange is near
When two legs trod the ice.

Timertik, big walrus is fat.
He dives in shallows to eat his fill.
Knows clams and sea worms
Make blubber thicken.

Timertik, big walrus is wily
Stays on floes far out in icy seas.
Knows how to hide when to flee.
But cannot hide forever.

Timertik, big walrus is prey.
I will take him with harpoon and lance.
Knows his death approaches
Then gives himself to me.

TATTOOING THE NEW BRIDE: BAFFIN ISLAND, CANADA 1896

The cod fish are cut in strips,
The ripe whale fluke is passed around.
The berries mixed with oil
The seal liver fried crisp and brown
Today we feast
In honor of the new bride's tattooing.

The house is hot and noisy
The many invited people crowd inside.
The smell of food and sweat mingle.
The laughter does not subside.
Today we feast
In honor of the new bride's tattooing.

The charcoal pot is ready
The needles flat to pierce her skin
The comments speak of her beauty
The lines of tattoo up and down her chin
Today we feast
In honor of the new bride's tattooing.

The young girls sit and watch
The faces plain without tattoo line
The thoughts are of their future beauty
The tattoos that will come in time.
Today we feast
In honor of the new bride's tattooing.

HARVESTING DUCKS: HUDSON BAY, CANADA 1946

Watch closely, my sons, and learn through your eyes.
Time to harvest *igunak, nerlerk and kanguk*
The ducks, the geese from the south, who nest in our lands.

Watch closely, my sons, and see how flight feathers fall.
Time to harvest *igunak, nerlerk and kanguk.*
The ducks, the geese, flightless now must walk to water.

Watch closely, my sons, and learn to make the noose of hide.
Time to harvest *igunak, nerlerk and kanguk.*
The ducks, the geese, walk this same path to search out food.

Watch closely, my sons, see how I place the loops of line.
Time to harvest *igunak, nerlerk and kanguk.*
The ducks, the geese, will never pass above our line.

Watch closely, my sons, and listen to my quiet words.
Time to harvest *igunak, nerlerk and kanguk*
The ducks, the geese, will try to pass beneath the line.

Watch closely, my sons, watch and do as I do here.
Time to harvest *igunak, nerlerk and kanguk.*
The ducks, the geese, will be caught by our strangling loops

Watch closely, my sons, and see how I preserve the catch
Time to harvest *igunak, nerlerk and kanguk*
The ducks, the geese, fat and juicy will hang to dry.

When the darkness creeps across our land to seal us in winter
We will not fear hunger or worry about empty bellies
We will feast on our harvest.

The ducks, the geese, fat sweet meats, will flavor our stews
We will congratulate ourselves for time taken to watch and learn.
Time made to harvest the *igunak, nerlerk and kanguk!*

SONGS FOR THE WHITE FOX:
SAINT LAWRENCE, ISLAND, ALASKA 1952

SONG ONE

Small white-furred brother
Trotting through the drifts
Your head into the wind.

White brush of your tail
Waving against the gale
Black pebble eyes alert.

Coat of warmth, hoar-frosted
Shaking ice crystals free
You dart from drift to drift.

You stop and pose-stride
Poking your black nose deep
Pluck a lemming from the snow.

SONG TWO

In the month before the sun comes back
You slink about the edges of our camp.
Your white fur is prime and every hunter knows this.
Your winter coat is thick and you are beautiful to see

In the month before the sun comes back
You slink about the edges of our camp.
You look fat but beneath your precious fur you starve
A thin frame of slack skin and hungry bones shiver.

In the month before the sun comes back
You slink about the edges of our camp.
The gnawing-poverty you feel makes you careless
The hunters will take you easily in deadfalls.
And
I will wear your precious white warmth of fur
In a parka ruff about my face.

SONG THREE

When the snow lies deep and crusted
Hard with frozen spring snow.
There is no reason for you to go hungry,
White fox
So think!
You have keen ears to hear all sounds
You have eyes to pierce the mists
You have claws so sharp and curved
So go!
Go dig!
Have you forgotten the puffin chicks?
Remember, you buried them beneath the grasses
At the sea-bird cliff face among the rocks.
So go!
Go dig!
Dig out a feast of swarming lemmings
They squeak to you beneath the snow
Daring you to find them, pull them out.
Don't be foolish old white fox.
Enjoy the food you cached for this time
This starving time of slow-coming spring.
So go!
Go dig!
You have more to eat than I do!

SONG FOUR

White fox tell me of yourself.
Why do you haunt our camps?
Why do you tease our dogs?
Why do you chase away the ptarmigan?
Why do you spoil our dried foods?
Why are you so mischievous?
I have watched you follow the great white bear.
I have watched you steal his leavings.
I know you are a scavenger, a trickster
Don't you want to be more?
Don't you want to be lordly like Nanuk, the bear?
Or are you happier just being a mischievous fox who haunts our camp?

NANNUK! NANNUK!: CHURCHILL MANITOBA, CANADA 1957

Nannuk! Nannuk!
Go away!
Let the little children come out to play!

I call you.
I have sung you my song four times now.
Do you not hear me
Do you not listen?

Grandfather says
Your kind foul the shores with waste we leave.
Me, I have seen this.
Why do you do it?

Grandmother says
You might take children like the dogs you kill.
Go hunt the shore seals.
Far away from here.

My father says
You bring tourists to watch while you linger here.
They frighten the game.
Our larder is bare.

Nannuk! Nannuk!
Go away!
Let the little children come out to play

My mother says
This is your home; you have a right to prowl.
You claimed all this place
Before *Inuk* came.

Here is what I say.
Though their words may be true I cannot play.
Locked in our *Iglu*.
I see you out there.

Nannuk! Nannuk!
Go away!
Let the little children come out to play!

This also I say.
One of us does not belong here in Churchill.
I Think it is you!
But you think it's me!

I will sing my song.
Sing it soft or loud, sing it many ways.
(My mind is made up!)
I will sing it now!
(My chant has power.)
It will force you to go!
(My little drum is loud!)
Leave now! Go away!

Nannuk! Nannuk!
You must go away!
because
The children of this village need to come out to play!
All children must play!
All children must play!

NIVIAKSIAK, IF YOU MUST DIE:
TUKTOYAKTUK NW TERRITORIES 1928

It will be a girl.
This child I carry in my rounded belly.
It will be a girl, *Niviaksiak,* a baby girl.
It will be a girl baby,
and I shall keep her.
My husband will say no.
No, to the girl child I carry next to my heart.
"It must die!"
He will say:
"We do not live in a village.
There are no others to feed us.
Give me a son. A son grows.
Grows to be a hunter who will provide for us
Hunt for us in our old age."
It will be a girl.
I tell him this and he scowls at me.
Raises his fist as if to beat me again.
"A girl!"
He shouts.
"Another mouth to feed?
What of our survival?
A girl in this iglu would be useless."
I do not look down.
I look into his face, boldly!
Let him beat me.
Let him rail and rage.
It will be a girl,
This child next to my heart
This child I carry in my fat belly.
Niviaksiak, my baby daughter,
You will not die!
I say this in my thoughts,
Inside my head and heart
So my baby girl will hear me.
To my husband I say,
I want to keep the girl!
It will be a girl, I know it! I know it I know it!

And
She will not go to the ice.
She will not die,
She will live.
My baby girl. My baby.
My *Niviaksiak*.
My life with you ends, husband, if she dies.
My life on this earth ends
The day you try to set her on the ice.
If I am gone,
Gone from this world,
Your life ends, too, husband.
No one will cook for you.
No one will make you clothing.
You will die.
You will starve and freeze.
Give me my baby girl's life.
Let my *Niviaksiak* live!
I have earned her.
Say it!
Say now that I shall keep the girl!
Say that she will live!

BLADDER FEAST: NUNIVAK ISLAND, ALASKA, 1860

In the men's house
the painted bladders hang.
Up there,
high near the smoke hole.

The time of cold
is here on the land outside.
The moon,
issraaciaq-taatqiq, hovers

Inside the men's house,
this *Karigi* we sweat
beside
great driftwood fires.

New food dishes of wood
The women have brought
To eat
fine feasts for us.

Two of us younger ones
have swept the *Karigi* it is
clean now
Evil and sickness tossed outside.

The spirits of ancestors
The food given by the Little girls.
Are fed
We dance our new songs.

All day the hunting stories
When the last song ends,
Tonight
So, will end our fasting.

The clubs and spears,
stand against the walls.
up-right
Wild parsnips tied at their tips.

The others ready their drums
Those who painted bladders
still fast.
and the round lamp-frame is hung.

Two hunters have gone out
to the sea ice to make a hole
Ice firm,
their labor will be great and long

The parsnip stalks and grass
are burned. and smolder now
We follow
the hunters to the ice
We circle the hole they have made.

We sing the hunting songs
the *inua*, the souls of the hunted
we honor
and return their bladder-souls to the sea

We race around the men's house
We sweep badness away
We chase
the evil-bearing spirits outside.

Now the Bladder Feast is ended.
The dead ancestors have been honored
We laugh
The animal souls set free

Tomorrow, the laughter grows.
We dance the masques, we sing.
We laugh
We run and we laugh.

CHANTS SUNG ALONG THE NOATAK: NOATAK RIVER, ALASKA 1940–1966

FAR AWAY

Away I go!
Far.
Far away
Far, far will I go
Away beyond those high hills!
Aja aja ajajai!
Aja aja ajajai!

Away I go!
Far.
Far away
Far, far will I go
Away to the land where birds live!
Aja aja ajajai!
Aja aja ajajai!

Away I go!
Far
Faraway
Far, far will I go
Away to the land over yonder!
Aja aja ajajai!
Aja aja ajajai!

WHEN THE SUN COMES BACK

This is what makes happiness.
Happiness in the heart.
This is what brings joy
Brings joy to the soul.
Feel it!
Feel the warmth
Come!
Warmth comes now into the great world.
The sun comes back
His old footsteps across the sky he follows.
He brings the summer nights of light.
The sun brings happiness and joy!

THE HUNTERS RETURN

Can you see them?
Can you see them?

Those men who come!
Those men who come!

Approaching in the distance.
Approaching in the distance.

Dragging beautiful seals!
Dragging beautiful seals!

Once more we feast!
Once more we feast!

The time of abundance sits in our land.
The time of abundance sits in our land.

Be thankful and laugh with me!
Be thankful and laugh with me!

FOOD CHANT

Look down and see me.
Here I stand.
Here I stand.
See my outstretched arms
See how I humble myself
I speak to you with gratitude
for the food.
For the food you will let sink down to me
O, great spirits of the air!

A WORK SONG

I am always at hand.
I am always at hand ready to help you.
I am eager for work.
I am eager and willing to work.
Show me the task
Show me the task I must do to help you.
I will do gladly.
I will do gladly, whatever needs to be done.
I am always at hand.
I am always at hand ready to help you.

I AM RESTLESS

The summer winds have set me in motion
The summer winds who shake the scrub willows and calls them to dance.

The summer sea, free of ice, has set me in motion
The summer sea who teases the shore and whispers to small stones.

The wide river in summer has set me in motion
The wide river in summer who moves the weeds in the water.

My feet are restless.
They want to wander, keep moving and take me away yonder.
My eyes are restless
They scan the horizon and watch the distant high hills far away.
Tomorrow I travel.
Tomorrow I will leave this place, but where will I go?

A WOMAN'S CHANT

We feast tonight.
The ceremonies begin.
Bring me my hair ornaments my pins of ivory and bone
With them,
I will make myself appealing to the strong young men.

CHANT OF THE OLD WOMEN SITTING IN THE SUN

Far to the south to the land of the sun
Far to the south of those who live south of us,
my soul has gone.
Gone to fetch warmth to last me the year 'round.
If you ask where my soul has gone
I will tell you this,
Follow me to the sun-warmed place
Help me fetch back my soul
and
the warmth of the sun.

IN AWE OF STORMS

The sky arches above me
Heavy and black!
The rains pelt the earth
Driving and hard!
The winds thrash the scrubs
Wailing and harsh!
The mightiness of such storms as these
Carries me away
Until
I am trembling with joy and fear.

CHANT OF THE OLD MEN SITTING IN THE SUN

Sitting here in the warm
I think of my youth.
I think of the early spring days of my youth.
An old man, seeking strength in his youth,
Loves most to think of the deeds that made him renown.
Was I ever that strong?
Was I ever that quick?
Was I ever such a lover of women?
Was I the hunter I thought I was?
Look at me now! What am I in the winter of my age?

A CHANT FOR MORNING

Quickly,
I arise from my mat.
I put the night's rest behind me.
Moving swiftly as the raven on wing
I will rise up quietly
and
Greet the day!

A CHANT FOR CASH MONEY

Come to my gun-sight, *Nanuk*, white bear.
You are cash money!
Fall under the stone of my sling, *Nappatak*, fox.
You are cash money!
Slip into my deadfall *Kakortok*,white lynx.
You are cash money.
I need cash money but how can I get it?
Only by hunting!
Only by Hunting!
I must shoot old white bear, kill the fox and trap lynx
If I get skins, I get dollars
Cash money for skins
Catch nothing
then
No cash money!

LOVE SONG

I am sitting here.
Alone I sit. I am sitting still.
In the distance
I see two kayaks approaching where I am sitting still.
Here I am.
sitting still with two men coming to court me.
They think I am easy and a ne'er-do-well
and
not so very good looking at that.
So why are they coming to court me?
Well, I have a surprise for them!
I will simply say, NO!

SONG FOR THE HIGH TIDE AT THE MOUTH OF THE RIVER

The sea is bewitched.
The river-mouth is bewitched.
All about us, all we see is bewitched.
Skin boats rise up on their moorings.
The water weeds drown below them.
Skin boats groan, their fastenings squeak
Earth itself hovers watching the tides.
Gulls and terns suspend flight, stand in the air,
hang loose on the air.
All around us is bewitched
when the tide turns.

BIG WINDS ARE BLOWING

My parka is flapping
The wolf ruff blinds my eyes.
Over the mountain
A black cloud is hovering.
I should have noticed the change in the light.
Mountain winds blow hard against my face.
The mountain, *Kissimelaq,*
the one we call "Stands by Itself" sends big winds
trying to blow me away.
Big winds tear at my parka, push me along paths
where I don't want to go.
That black cloud tried to warn me!
I should have listened.

A CHANT FOR THE SEALS

Aja Ja Japape
Hard times! Hard time plague us
Plague us everyone
See our shrunken stomachs, hear our crying babes.
Give yourselves to our hunters
Our dishes are empty.
Aja ja japape aja ja japape!

CHANT TO KEEP YOUR HUSBAND SAFE
WHILE HE HUNTS THE WHALES

My face is turned there.
My face is turned in that direction,
I will keep looking there.
I will keep looking in that direction.

My face is turned away from the dark of night
There, I do not gaze.
I will keep my gaze in the direction of the dawn
Toward the whiteness of the dawn.
I will not think of the dark
but
only think of the light.

A CHANT TO DISPELL SADNESS

I call forth this song
To ease my sorrow.
I draw a deep breath
My chest feels heavy
weighted with sorrow.
I call forth this song
I will throw this song out
across the sky I will throw it.
A song I call forth
A deep breath I draw
to throw out this song
across the sky I throw it.
Listen!
Aye aye aye aye!
Aye aye aye aye!

A CHANT SUNG WHILE COOKING

Do you know that smell?
Do you know the smell?
It is the smell of pots on the boil!
Do you know that smell?
Do you know that smell?
It is the smell of lumps of blubber!
Do you know that smell?
Do you know that smell?
It is the smell of fresh meat on the side bench!
Thank those who brought us this plenty.
Thank those who brought us this joy!
Come eat with us!
Come feast with us!
Come taste this plenty!

CHANT FOR PICKING SPRING GREENS

I love to go walking!
I love to go walking far and away
Until the soles of my *mukluks* are worn thin
And the moss water seeps through.
I love to go walking.
I love to go walking far and away,
To pluck the delicious young buds of willow.
They are furry and soft
Like the great he-wolf's beard.

CHANT FOR PROTECTION WHILE TRAVELING DOWN RIVER

Rarely do I see calm water,
so
River calm yourself!
Do not let your waves cast me about!
Be calm! Be calm!
Do not let me tremble so.
I tremble and I tremble
at
the thought of the hour when the gulls hack at my dead body
awash in the river tide.
River, great river, be calm!

OBSERVATIONS OF THE GREAT WHITE BEAR: ARCTIC COASTLINE

I.

ice creeper
master of stealth
mountain of patience
white death for seal
you wait
not moving
by the breathing hole
you wait.
I must copy your ways.

II.

I chase after danger,
even my own death, when I track you.
you walk ahead of me
your tracks, toe in, lead me to you.
If you know I follow
you seem not to care.
I will find you
and
let loose my dogs to surround you.
I will plant my lance against the ice when you rear up to charge me
and
I will take you.

III.

My tongue remembers.
My tongue remembers the taste of your flesh.
(A delicacy.)
My mind remembers.
My mind remembers the great mound of meat.
(Piled high in my cache).
My body remembers.
My body remembers the warmth of your hide.
(lying next to my wife)

IV.

Women,
when you skin this bear
when you
gut out this white bear
cut up his flesh only
and leave his liver.
leave it on the ice.
to eat Nannuk's liver is taboo.
your hair will fall out
and
you might die!

V.

My son,
When you hunt the white bear,
you must watch every hummock
every small hill of ice.
Often he waits there.
Hidden,
crouched in the snow.
You then are the hunted
and
he is the hunter.
Careful, my son, beware!
Look for his dark shadow;
black on the snow.
Then creep down-wind behind him
and become the hunter again

VI.

I cannot see you, dreaded bear.
but I know you are there.
Hidden in the blowing snow
You sound your dreaded roar.
Marking me your prey.
Have you learned the taste
of man's flesh?
Is that why you follow me?
On your way, Nannuk!
Go search for seals and leave me be!

VII.

This white bear I track is starving.
the toes of his tracks point inward.
His belly is empty he has no fat
to make his toes point out.

This white bear I track is starving,
Perhaps he is old and has no teeth.
His eyes may be blind to agile seals.
His great claws worn and blunted.

This white bear I track is starving.
Nannuk, I will follow you no more.
Nannuk, I will search for other food.
I, one day, will be old and worn-out and thin.
I pity you, Nannuk,
so go on your way.

VIII.

Clever one, Nannuk.
I admire your cleverness.
I saw you wait in silence on the bluff above the sea
Above the place where the walrus haul out to sun.
I noted your patience until the herd slept.
I saw you push the boulders from the high cliff
Tossing them down with your mighty paws
Crushing the skulls of the fat sleepy ones
I watched you feasting on blubber.
I would try this trick myself, but
clever Nannuk, I lack your strength.

IX

On the drifting ice!
There! A white bear.
It comes running toward me
Not to greet me like a playful puppy
but to eat me up.
I will fight this bear
Dodge its claws until it wearies
Then I will take it down with my lance!

INSTRUCTIONS FOR TAKING A SEAL: KOTZEBUE, ALASKA, 1952

I.

Be silent.
Stand quietly.
Watch always
Listen, listen
then
You will know when seal comes to his breathing hole.
then
will you take him.

II.

Take this.
It is my *Caller-of-Seals.*
On this wooden handle
I have attached the claws of seal.
Rake it on the ice.
Kneel before a breathing hole
Harpoon ready
Scrape the ice as seal does.
Caller-of-Seals will bring you meat!

III.

When you take a seal
Hold!
Do not take him
from the ice too quickly!
Reach into the water and feel the face.
If it has human features and long hair
Stop!
Cut the line and leave it.
Careful!
Perhaps it is a merman you captured.
Release it!
Or you will surely die!

THOSE WHO CAME BEFORE: SAINT LAWRENCE ISLAND, 1953

I dig
In the ruined mound of this old house.
I search the ruins for tools, old tools.
Tools. Ivory trinkets
The white man pays me good money
Cash money for these things
Made by the hands of those who came before.
Amulets of ivory
Harpoon sockets
Stone lamps.
I dig.
Today I find nothing.
I find only bones
Bones, old bones
Of a man who came before.
He is not offended
Now
That I have dug up his bones.
His spirit is gone
Only the bones and his memory remain.
His bones belong to the rodents
They carve designs on them with their small teeth.
His memory belongs to the people
They sing of him in songs
Each year
They sing honoring songs
For the ones who came before.
I dig
I dig in this ruined mound
Where
Only his carved bones remain
They are only dead bones
But his memory remains
This man who came before

SONG OF "POINTING FINGER", TIGARA: TIKIGAQ, POINT HOPE, ALASKA 1957

Here the wind blows.
Seldom does it stop.
It blows hard as if in anger
Never-ending, constant wind.
In this small village of Tigara,
Pointing Finger,
Pointing West, Tigara.

Here people dwell
Here they have always been.
Since beyond time
Since beyond the memories of all.
When Tigara came to be.
Our oldest ones cannot recall
Nor our father's nor their fathers

Here the wind blows.
Never does it stop.
It blows the ice floes out to sea
Brings open water all around.
Whales and winter seal are ours.
Our people feast
We have much oil for lamps

Here people dwell
Here they have always been.
Since beyond time
From the time before time
When Raven built the world
Here the wind blows.
Seldom does it stop.
Here in the village of the Tikeraqmiut.

QUESTIONS FOR A GRANDMOTHER

Ana, Grandmother
What do birds feel?
Do they feel jealous?
Does the gull envy the tern who can stand still in mid-air?

Ana, Grandmother
What do birds feel?
Do they know envy?
Does the snow-owl wish to swim like the Eider or loon?

Ana, Grandmother
What do birds feel?
Do they feel anger?
Does the ptarmigan want to steal Raven's wisdom?

Ana, grandmother
Why can't I know?
Why won't the birds answer my questions?
The language they speak is one I don't know.

TUFTED PUFFIN

Fat bodied bird,
Gawky in flight
You are a fisherman
I envy your skill.
Come fly to my nets
Entangle your head
I will stuff you in seal poke
use your beak for a jewel
My wife will make hair ties
Of your long yellow plumes

SPRING MIGRATION

The sky is full of snow geese
They fly day and night over our camp.
Stilt-legs and sandpipers cover tundra ponds.
The gulls and the auklets wheel over the cliffs
Quarrel with puffins for nesting space.
Abundant are the birds.
The moon of *Irniivik* passes
The fawns have been born
The eiders return
Now comes *Mannit*,
the moon of eggs

MUKLUKS

Snowy owl walks across the snow
He does not feel the cold
He does not slip or slide.
Ptarmigan climbs icy willows
Wades into the snow
He does not feel cold
Like the snowy-owl
He has feathered mukluks on his feet!

SEARCHING FOR DUCKS

Look carefully among the dry pond rushes.
Search diligently in tufts of tundra grass.
The eider ducks cannot fly now
They have dropped their feathers.
Set your snares with care among dry rushes
Search driftwood beach where they hide
Catch them! Catch them!
We will eat their tasty flesh
Make fine soup of their bones
We will wear the warmth of soft down
Against our bodies when winter cold comes

THE LOON ON OUR POND

That bird out there
The loon
on our pond
keeps me from needed sleep.
Clever diver
wary bird with necklaced throat
Your noise steals my sleep.
Groans,
you groan like one suffering
You shriek
like a woman in pain
You laugh
like a drunken man
or a young girl, embarrassed
Dive
Dive to the bottom of the pond
Stay there
and let me sleep.

WATCHING MOULTING DUCKS

Are you ashamed?
Is that why you hide
by day, safe,
in grassy caves
along the banks of the pond?
Ashamed
That you cannot fly?
You trip
over your own flat feet
you waddle out at dusk
to search
for bits of food.
Quacking
In hushed tones
You scurry back and forth
as brief night comes.
Timid ducks,
Once such proud birds.
Now so ashamed

SEA BIRDS

Out on the sea
amid the small ice flows
the tiny shifting ice islands
are rafts of sea birds.
They twitter and call to each other
in shrill high voices.
When we approach in our skin boat
they shriek out alarms.
Fly as a unit on whirring wings
up into the sky
but briefly.
Settling down amid the little ice flows,
not too far
from where we paddle,
they begin their twittering conversations again.

GEESE

Some say geese are silly
That they are fools among birds
Because they sometimes act foolish
Does not mean they always are.
Often they come too early to nest
There is nothing green to eat.
Sometimes they follow each other
The first in a row
Leads the others to danger.
Perhaps it is true
They abandon their egg nests
And then build another
I have watched geese.
I have watched people.
I have watched our people do as geese do
Some *Kabloonak* say our people are silly
Because we do not do they, white men, do
Say that our people are fools among fools
Because they sometimes act foolish
Does not mean our people always are

WHO SANG THAT SONG: YUPIK, KOTZEBUE SOUND, ALASKA 1952

I went north
North,
far from our village
Hunting the bearded seal.
I prayed
Prayed,
for success in my hunting
It was Spring
Spring
when the days are long
I walked
Walked
along my eyes searching
I heard
Heard,
the voice of a man singing
I found it
Found,
the place from where the song came
I saw it
Saw,
In the distance a high ice ridge.
I hurried there
Hurried to the ice ridge.
I listened
Listened,
to the song the man sang.

> *"I am sitting here, sitting here*
> *sitting in the sun*
> *enjoying the warm sun*
> *enjoying the warmth of the sun*
> *where it strikes this ice ridge"*

I waited
Waited,
until the song was finished
I crept
Crept,
Around the edge of the ice ridge.

I looked there
Looked,
For the singer of the song
I saw nothing
Saw,
No man was there behind the ice ridge
Only
only a bearded seal slipped quickly into the sea.
I wonder
Wonder,
will always wonder
Who sang that song

SONG OF THE WHALE CAPTAIN'S WIFE: YUPIK, TIGARA 1880

Dweller of the moon
Great and powerful dweller of the moon
Dweller of the moon
High above me in the blue-black sky
Dweller of the moon
Generous and great giver of whales
Please, hear me.
It is I, *Nivasiarnuna,* wife
of a young new whaler of Tigara
He is an eager man and he is hopeful
He needs your help.
Dweller of the moon
I implore you
Send him the life-giving thing he seeks
Dweller of the moon
I beseech you
Dweller of the moon
Give my husband a fine great whale
Dweller of the moon,
Great and powerful one
I, *Nivasiarrnuna,* wife
Of this young new whaler
I beg you be generous
You know our people need to live

UNALASKA, ALASKA: 1957

Home of the storm maker
Home of the fog maker
Home of the raging winds
Blue and grey
Blue and grey
Sunless place of storms
Sunless land of treeless mountains
Here rain and snow blow sideways
Here the thick fog obscures my feet
Out there icy Bering water
Out there warm *Kuroshio* meet to breed storms
Here the weather changes too fast
Here all is unpredictable:
Unexpected
earthquakes and tidal waves
Here life is hard
And
Here I fear to live.

NIKOLSKI, ALEUTIAN ISLANDS, ALASKA, 1957

Have you seen the sea birds?
The sky is speckled with them
Their cries bring pain to your ears
Out there on those islands of the four mountains
Fulmars and puffins
Murres, kittiwakes and cormorants
Mass on the islands
Hundreds of millions
Have you seen the animals?
Hauled out on the beach ledge
Barking and brawling
A brown mat on the rocks of the islands out there
Fur seals and sea lions
In numbers uncountable
In the kelp beds
Otters
Wrapped tight in the fronds
Bobbing safe in the waves, challenging the storm
Watching the great whales slip through the channels
Grey monsters bound north.

MEMORIES OF ATTU: ALEUTIAN ISLANDS, ALASKA 1983

No one told us
No one told us they would come
No one told us
No one told us we would be prisoners
in the far land of Hokkaido
No one told us of Japan
No one told us our beautiful island would suffer
No one told us
No one told us our island would know death's touch
Or of the soldiers who would die here
Thousands from America how many from Japan
No one told us
our island would be scarred
Pock-marked with craters
Ruined land
Evidence of bombs and mortars
No one told us of an island
riddled with trenches
Hastily dug
like the graves of the dead
Homes to the ghosts of both warring sides
No one told us
No one told us we would later be interned
The government
Forced us to the canneries
No one told us why.
No one told us we would die there
No one told us of the hunger and humiliation
we were forced to endure
No one told us that we would die.
No one told us
No one told us when we finally returned
the ghosts of our elders
would be forced to share their homeland
with the soldier-ghosts
already there

BEFORE THE STRANGERS CAME: ALEUTIAN ISLAND CHAIN: 1550

We found these islands
These islands anchored in this rainy sea of fog.
We came here,
took this land as our home.
We saw the abundant seas all around
We took the sea's bounty
and lived well.
Our woman were beautiful to look upon
And our young men stalwart.
In skin boats we skimmed the waves as we hunted
Gave thanks for our bounty
in song and dance.
Our elders knew medicines to ease our sickness
Our medicine people knew how to cut out disease and sew the wounds
Our dead we honored with mummification.
We thrived
We advanced from island to island
Our might and our people
both grew.
Then they came in the great boats with cloth sails
The strangers with their death-sticks called guns.
We were no match for the *promyshleniki*
This name they gave themselves we learned to fear.
We fought for our land
Defeated we were enslaved
Our elders were the first to die: our ways died with them
Our medicine people driven out
Our songs and dances forgotten
Nothing remained
We became a people without direction.
A people without life
What such people can do to live again
To become again
we must soon discover

TO EAT WELL: UMNAK ISLAND, ALEUTIANS, 1960

In summer
At the summer camp
in our barabara house
half buried in the hillside
we eat well!
Everywhere the green
surrounds us
The mist and rain
bring out the plants for our table
fresh greens and roots
ground berries well hidden
We eat well!
in summer
at the summer camp
When the tide is out
the table is set
A banquet for us
at low tide
clams, the mussels quick octopus
and crab
In the gill nets exposed by the tide
salmon hang helpless
We eat well!
in summer
at the summer camp
You must visit us
to eat well.
We will wait for the tide to go out
then our table is set!

CHILD OF THE ALUTIIQ: NIKOLSKI, ALEUTIAN ISLANDS 1970

Hear tell they'll close the school.
No little children here anymore.
Except me
and four others.
That's good
Closing the school.
I like learning
don't like indoors school.
I'm eleven
Almost a man.
How can I learn men things
Inside a wooden box school.
I need to hunt
I want to trap and catch salmon.
I need to know the beach
Find rock caves where octopus hides
Search sea rocks jeweled with mussels
Seek best place for my crab pot.
I need to know these things.
Alutiiq things.
They don't teach all this
In school, so
It's good they'll close the school
Then I can learn
Learn to be a man
Outdoors
Like a good Alutiiq.

TRAVELLING WITH ME: UMNAK, ALEUTIAN ISLANDS 1970

I'll show you the hills
Treeless and greener than green
I'll show you the beaches
Hidden and pebbled
I'll show you the sea-caves and rocks
Secret and glistening
You must travel with me in this mist of rain
You must travel with me
walking to these places in the grey rain.
Walking mile after mile in the
whipping mist of this constant rain
Travelling with me to see them.

CALDERA: UMNAK ISLAND, ALEUTIAN CHAIN, 1980

Beneath the sea
Fire lives.
Molten fire seeps to the surface
Warming earth
Forcing growth
Things green
Unexpected
Abound here.
Surreal
Moonscape from past time
Fumarole fields
Smoking
Steaming
Belching foul breath
Into cover of low clouds and mist.
Smell of sulfur or
Eggs gone bad
Fantastic fire carved Okmok
Crater of surprises
Graceful mount of Vsevidorf
Silent now
Waiting
To birth fire and ashes
Ring of fire
Mountains of flame
Bring us
Unexpected delights
Hot springs
Muddy water
Hot water
Restoring baths
Welcome and needed
For centuries
Bathing place of Alutiiq
Partov Cove
Thermal wonderland
Volcano land

BAD WOMAN OF THE SEA: ARCTIC COAST 1850

she owns the fog
clammy and cold
she owns the winds
southwest winds
blowing danger
when she passes
the sea is restless
under the waves
she owns all things
she commands the animals
offended by misdeeds
she keeps the sea animals
hidden in the bowl
of her great lamp
Her stone lamp
deep under the water
offended by misdeeds
she has summoned
walrus and seals
great whales
white whales
to hide in her lamp
the fish do not swim
sea birds do not fly
all at her command
because
because someone
has offend *Nivikkaah*
Nivikkaah! Nivikkaah!
Bad Sea-Woman
until amends are made
our village is idle
kayaks cannot venture
on angry seas
the people
know fear and hunger
these two are our
constant companions

THE LESSONS OF THINGS: ARCTIC CIRCLE VILLAGE, ALASKA 1937

Grandmother says
Learn the lessons of the earth
Grandmother says
Learn the ways of all creatures.
Grandmother says
Watch the changing of the river
Grandmother says
Watch the winds where they blow

My Father says
Learn the cycle of split-hooves
My Father says
Learn the habits of geese
My Father says
Learn the summer dance of the hare
Learn where animals hide

Grandfather says
Learn the paths on the land
Grandfather says
Seek the knowledge of trees
Grandfather says
Watch snowy owl hunting
Grandfather says
Learn to follow the lynx

My Mother says
Learn where loons lay their eggs
My Mother says
Learn where molting ducks hide
My Mother says
Learn to walk with bears
My Mother says
Learn the lessons of things.
I say there are so many lessons

ANGATKRO: KIDLINERMIUT MAC KENZIE RIVER REGION, YUKON TERRITORY, CANADA

Things hidden to us
A Shaman can find
Things unseen
A Shaman can see
Angatkro, Shaman,
You guard well your secrets
Lesser men cannot fly to the moon
Angatkro, Shaman,
You run with the wolf
Borrow his spirit
You call to the air spirits
Then fly with the birds
You see afar
You read our dreams
Speak with *Sedna* undersea
Angatkro, Shaman,
You are friend to ghosts
Conspirator with the dead
I would not care
To be like you!

SHARING JOY: INUPIAT, KAKTOVIK, ALASKA 1928

Inupiat mouths long to sing songs
Inupiat feet want to stomp in a dance
Inupiat hands want to tell old stories
Inupiat arms want to beat loud drums
Inupiat smiles want to become laughter
Inupiat hearts want to share joy

SUMMER'S END: INUPIAT, KAKTOVIK, ALASKA 1929

Frost came last night
Now
Grasses and pond weeds droop
Skeins of geese wing the skies
Southbound.
With other birds
Who have gone before
Tundra ponds lay silent and cooled
No loons call
Nests are all empty
Summer life has fled.
Autumn will follow.

I sit here alone
My face turned to the south
Begging warmth from fading sun
My house is empty
My children flown away
Like new-fledged goslings
Like tundra ponds
My blood lays cool and silent
In my withering breast
My summer is gone
But my life has not fled.
Perhaps I will learn
To accept
The autumn of my life.

ON BECOMING A MAN: KING ISLAND, ALASKA, 1860

Here on our rocky island
a boy
who was ready becomes a man
Tonight
in the council house he will become a man
This once scrawny boy, now handsome and strong
who used to squeak
like a lemming
now has a wolf's low growl.
His eyes notice the women
They smile at him
eyes lowered
coy and inviting,
But he is not yet a true man.
First his boyish clothes
will be taken
His hair cut
His head even shaved.
Next his mouth will be prepared
for the labrets of a man.
Held in the vice
of an elder's knees
His head will be tilted
His chin exposed to the stone blade
The cuts will be made
The boy-man
remains silent utters no cry
Round knobs
Small, polished wood
pushed through the slits
at the corners of his mouth
The blood comes and drips
on his naked legs
The women wipe
the wounds with urine soaked moss
All make sounds of honor
and praise
admiring his courage
Slowly he stands, the new man of our people
Hunter and father to be.

THE LAND OF THE LONG SHADOWS: ARCTIC REGIONS

Land of long shadows
Land of the long springtime
Land of awesome beauty
My land, my home

Land of simple forms
Land of sea, plain and mountain
Land of subtle colours
My land, my home

Land of eternal summer light
Land of endless dark winter
Land of fragile existence
My land, my home

Land of sudden wild blooms
Land of hasty seeding and flourishing
Land of sun-quickened life too quickly dead
My land, my home

Land of high odds and little to chance
Land never yielding hostile to man
Land of my father's ways carefully crafted
My land, my home

Land of peoples not remembered
Land of millennia older than time
Land vulnerable more fragile than any
My land, my home

LIVING THE GOOD LIFE UNDER THE BROOKS RANGE:
ANAKTUVUK PASS, ALASKA, 1990

We have a good life here
Now that the pipeline's gone through
The oil-men helped us
Gave us the good life
But didn't plan to.

No more tar-paper shacks
Since the Borough came through
Gave us all that money
Dumped it all in our laps
Told us what to do

Built us a school house
With all that state money
Got us nice houses
Mine's two stories but
Didn't cost me a penny

Got us a satellite TV
With that dish high on the mountain
We can watch wrestlin' and hockey
Order stuff on line
And have it flown in

Let Barrow tax the oil rigs
And let's just keep 'em pumpin'
We're living the good life
And I tell you, brother,
that sure is somethin'

Things sure have changed
Since the year we begun
Lived chasin' the caribou
When my daddy was spry
That was back in 1951

Got us a pool hall
Costs five dollars to play
But wages is high about two hundred
A day working construction
That's good times, I'd say.

It costs me a bundle
To care for wife and kids
Milk's seven dollars a gallon
Six hundert a month for fuel
Hope things don't go on the skids.

So with the pipeline
North Slope Borough and all
Construction is boomin'
The money rolls in but
Some folks is predictin' a bust and fall

Yeah the money rolls in with a capital "M"
But when the buildin is finished
The good life could fade
The boom's gotta end
You'd better be ready
To chase caribou again.

SUMMER WEDDING: DOGRIB VILLAGE, RAE LAKES, CANADA, 1983

Three in the morning
Hour of the fox
Smoke from a dozen campfires
Blue-hazed air
Feeble light of midnight sun
Children huddle
Sleep-eyed and worn
Smudge-pots
Smoldering
Thickening the air
Driving out
Hissing
Mosquito clouds.
A wedding
Double wedding
Two brothers and brides
Married at midnight
Hour of the owl
Old ceremonies
Old chants
Joined the pairs
They sit together
A place of honor
While others
Gossip about them.
Hour of the muskrat
Fat feasting
On rabbit, moose
Geese and hare
The new brides are restless
The hours drag on
New husbands
Eager impatient
Wait for the throng
To disperse
But they linger
Hour of the raven
Nothing to do
Nowhere to go
Easy summer life
Makes Dogribs lazy
This morning
Sleep is optional

broad river of my people
winding looping
curving back to watch yourself
slipping past to the sea
through flat land
a tundra tapestry
of ponds and lakes
mosquitoed pot holes
with mountains behind you
hurrying then slowing
flowing north
you leave stunted trees behind
dwarf willows grow
a scraggly green beard
along your banks
here the great forests dwindle
beyond lies the Inuit lands
white cold haunting
in your patchwork of coiled channels
the dying forest takes
a last breath
scruffy spruce burrow deep
seeking life-water
in the troughs
of your frozen streams
then
the willows are gone
replaced by infinite whiteness

LESSONS OF THE DOMINANT CULTURE: INUIT, REPULSE BAY, 1982

So white
So bright
So correct
So right
Lessons in the dominant culture

Inuit children
In your new school
Government school
You are taught these lessons

Kindergarten
First grade to grade three
Subtle lessons
Learned behaviors

So white
So bright
So correct
So right
Lessons of the dominant culture

Little *Inuit* girl
Playing with white-skinned doll
Of yellow hair sky-coloured eyes
Subconscious lesson

In this school
Inuktitut, your mother's tongue
You still speak
Next year a foreign tongue

So white
So bright
So correct
So right

Remember little *Inuit* children
Learn the lessons of the dominant culture
Make sure you learn them well.
Success is still spelled in English

SEPERATED TWINS: THE DIOMEDES, ALASKA AND SIBERIA 1947

Remnants of a land bridge
our ancestors trod
you huddle in the shallow sea
facing each other
staring
across the short space of water
yearning for contact again
you are divided twins
one on the edge of yesterday
the other
the start of tomorrow
Big Diomede
Little Diomede
you live in a different day
a different world
but
the people who walk your lands
are one

ARCTIC LOVE SONG: ARCTIC RIM 1952

my people are of the Tundra
I wish to be among them
I dream of one day
one day when I meet someone
someone who will be the subject of my love
the Tundra is so wide
and one must look far
but in time
I will find him

PICKING BERRIES; KOTZEBUE SOUND, ALASKA 1950

Picking berries
Up on the grassland near the bluff
I looked out to sea.
My relatives
They were coming in a skin boat
I shaded my eyes
For sure
They were coming
Across the flat water of the sound
Many people
Crowded into one big umiak.
I felt happy
Visitors and relatives were always welcome
More berries.
I would need more berries for a feast
A feast
For my relatives.
Food for relatives and visiting friends
With lowered head
I bent down
My eyes searching for many minutes
When I stood up
I looked out to sea
Grief rushed into my heart
Fear entered my blood
Out there
On the flat water of the sound
The boat
Overturned
Tilted in the water
Tiny doll-figures struggled to hold on
I screamed
The wind took my cries and blew them inland
No one heard
No one saw but me
Alone on the bluff high up
Picking berries
My grief over came me
My legs failed me
I fell to the ground among the berries.

Later I came back to myself
Sour fear taste filled my mouth
My heart drummed
Too fast
My throat was tight closed
I shaded my eyes with my berry stained hand
Scanned the sea
The umiak was gone
The doll-figures were gone
Gone beneath the sea to Sedna's land
Never again will I see my relatives and friends
I cannot eat berries ever after that time
I do not go to the high bluff
With the other women.
I tried once
But my old grief overcame me.

MUTUAL DISCOVERIES:
JOHN ROSS EXPIDITION, POLAR REGIONS 1819

When first we saw their great ships
We pointed to the flapping sail-wings
We asked
What great creatures are these?
We asked
Do they come from the sun or the moon?
We asked
Do they shine with the light of the day
Or are they creatures of the night?
When we first saw their pale skins
We covered our mouths and laughed.
We asked
Are you ghosts so pale and tall?
We asked
Were your fathers dogs to give you such hairy faces?
We asked
Many questions,
Many times, many times over
but these strangers
these hairy white ghosts
could not speak the language
of the real people,

When we first saw them, the savages
these eaters of raw flesh
we were surprised indeed
by their round faces
by their swarthy skins
we asked
What place have we come to?
We asked
What name do you call yourselves?
Do you recognize white men
Do you have food supplies to trade?
When we first encountered their grimy persons
We were amused at their childlike ways
We asked
Will you trade? Where are your women?
We asked
Many questions
Many times, many times over
But these savages
These dirty brown men
Could not speak the language
Of intrepid Englishmen

ANERNERK: ARCTIC RIM GREENLAND 1820

Breath cannot be seen
except when the cold
surrounds it
Breath comes from our mouths
like fog in winter
Breath taken from us
brings death.
Words cannot be seen
except when white men
write them down
Words tumble from our mouths
like melt-water from spring ice
Words spoken
are gone forever
Both breath and words
melt away
like sea fog.

KABLOONAK: BAFFIN ISLAND, CANADA 1830

When the Kabloonak came
The white men we named
For their big eyebrows and hairy faces
When they came we thought them truthful men
Like us, the real people, *Inuk*
But now, after eight summers
Living among us
We know they cannot speak the truth.
Their lies are many and amusing
They spin splendid tales
Grander
More imaginative than our children tell
Hairy big-browed Kabloonak
They entertain us with their lies
So we listen.
They say they come from the other side of the world
Where all men have hairy faces.
Their fathers are dogs, we know
But they lie about this to us.
The Kabloonak say there
Are mountains there so high a man cannot cross
We smile at this tale
They say,
But we do not believe them,
The sun shines and cold does not come to their land
How foolish this lie
They say things grow in the earth called trees.
With round balls of sweetness they call fruit.
We pretend to believe them and their fruit.
They say there is never a long night
They say the sea never freezes
They entertain us with their lies
So we listen
But
do not believe a single Kabloonak tale

SING A SONG OF ENVY:
ARCTIC BIRDS TUNDRA REGIONS, ALASKA 1952

water bird
water bird
duck of the long tail
duck with rings on your face
duck with white eye
Is it fun
Is it fun
to duck under water
into the wet water
bobbing under and down
air spirit
air spirit
bird of forked tail
black and white sprite, hovering
you never fly fast
is it fun
is it fun
to hang in midair
in cool summer air
white bird
white bird
feathers on your feet
changing coats with the seasons
willow-bud bird
is it fun
is it fun
sleeping under the snow
when fox comes hunting
water bird
air spirit
white bird under the snow
is it fun
is it fun
I'm only a boy
Tell me
or
I'll never know

SHE WHO SURVIVED: SAMUEL HEARNE EXPEDITION, UNCHARTED TUNDRA LANDS, CANADA 1772

mid-winter
desolate tundra
wind-scoured nothingness
white upon whiteness never ending
the tracks
a single line track
one snowshoe leading away
in the distance a shelter of skins
a woman
young, sitting alone
in her miserable shelter-dome
of hurriedly patched-together skins
she smiled
when we found her
offered us thin watery broth
from a tiny pot
copper pot of the Indians
she spoke
our Inuit guide
interpreted her story
she was the sole survivor
of a family
husband, mother and father and infant child
all killed by Kutchin Indians
seven months she has hurried north
leaving the killers behind
they did not follow
worthless woman
they thought
but she survived.
it is curious how she managed
in spite of her forlorn situation
to be so well composed of mind
her garments, her boots, all she had created for herself
on this seven months journey to freedom
had served her well
but more than that
her fur clothing,
crudely but cleverly made for real service

was generously decorated
with intricate patterns of coloured skins.
and bits of tiny bleached bone
which were very pleasing to the eye
when our Inuit guide presented my query
why?
why did you create such beauty
in the face of such hardship and possible death
when you should have been concerned
only for things absolutely essential?
she answered simply:
My soul demanded it.
it was then I knew,
without further explanation,
just how she had survived.

SONGS FOR A WALRUS KILL:
SAINT LAWRENCE ISLAND, ALASKA 1952

SONG ONE

I will whisper the right words
I will make prayers for you
I will call your name softly
Great beast of the sea
Come here to my lance
Come offer yourself
In the early pink light

Hear my prayer and my plea
Great beast of the sea
Whispered into the morning air
For your ears only
These are sacred words I whisper
Full of power and charm
I know not their power
Their mysterious power
But I know these words
Will bring you to me.

SONGS FOR A WALRUS KILL:
SAINT LAWRENCE ISLAND, ALASKA 1952

SONG TWO

This night
This long nighttime
I could not sleep
Outside my house
The sea lay flat
Calm and smooth
I could not resist
I rowed out
You walrus,
Came up close
beside my kayak
surprised
I thrust my lance
into your side
harpoon head fast
the bobbing
sealskin float bounced
flew over the water.
You surfaced
Angry
Tried to tear the float
Rend it in pieces
Your strength
Was spent
In this foolishness
For inside the float
The skin of a lemming
An unborn lemming
Was sewn
A charm
A guardian amulet
For me
And my float
I sing this song
I sing it loud
Because
All men in our village
Who take a walrus
Fill their songs
With self-praise

SONG MAKER:
NORTH EAST CAPE, SAINT LAWRENCE ISLAND, ALASKA 1953

There is great joy
There is great joy
In making songs

A wonderful thing
A wonderful thing
Is making songs

Pleasant occupation
Pleasant occupation
The making of songs

But all too often
But all too often
They are failures
Aja aja aja aie!
Aja aja aja aie!

FACES OF FRIENDS: TIGARA, ALASKA 1951

Faces
Dear faces
Sweet faces of friends
The hills are more beautiful
The land is more beautiful
My dwelling is more beautiful
When I can see
Faces
Dear faces
Sweet faces of friends
All around me is more beautiful
All around me is more beautiful
My heart is so full
My heart is so full
Thankful am I
Thankful am I
When I see
Faces
Dear faces
Sweet faces of friends
These guests who come
Make my house so beautiful.

THEN AFTER THAT, WHERE DO THEY GO?: NOME, ALASKA 1957

I watch the sun
Coming into my world
Bringing warmth
I watch the sun
Follow it's old path across the sky
Tracing the same footsteps
In the summer afternoon
Then
After that
Where does he go?

I watch the moon
Seeing the new moon, then full moon
Dancing her dance across the night sky
Dancing the same ancient dance
In the summer night
Then
After that
Where does she go?

I watch the cold
Creeping back to my world
Chilling the land
I watch the cold
Capturing the landscape around me
Staying too long
Then
After that
Where does it go.

I watch the elders
Sitting so silent sadly so calm
Remembering their memories
Sighing and staring into the lamp
Leaving us, dying
Then
After that
where do they go?

SPRINGTIME: CHEVAK, ALASKA 1953

When brother sun
lingers above the horizon
things in Chevak change
All the girls
the young women
start to gather in little flocks
Then these little groups
they go from house to house
paying nonsense visits
The girls dress in smiles
and fancy new
flower-print parkas
Then all at once
the men want to be manly
The girls simply smile
and think of sweet lies to tell us.

MOURNING SONG: KING ISLAND, ALASKA 1939

You were right to go
You were right to leave us
Dear brother-friend

You were right to go
You were right to leave us
Now you do not want.

In the place you are
In that land beyond
Things are better for you

Here we must sing a sad song
This land is poor
Poor it is
This ice is poor
Poor it is
This air is poor
Poor it is
This sea is poor
Poor it is
This life is poor
Poor it is

IN MY WAY OF THINKING: A LEADER'S REMARKS, KOTZEBU, 1989

This thing called civilization
Is not a gift, is not a prize
It is something we must work at
Something we must polish and preserve
Other civilizations
There have been many
They have come and they have gone
The past is strewn with the relics of such civilizations
Gone and long forgotten
Because they lost their identity
We, the people, Yupik people
Have identity
We must strive not to loose it
We must work
to polish and preserve
If we succeed
The world will remember
It is worth the struggle
If we fail as a people
We deserve to disappear

LOWER FOURTH AVENUE: ANCHORAGE, ALASKA 1962

In the hallways
In the doorways
Or outside in the alley
Against the dumpster
Frozen bodies
Derelicts and lost souls
From villages far to the north
Searched the bars for kin and friends
They did not find
Drink themselves
Into pain-free stupor
With each shot of whiskey
The heart-pangs and homesickness lessens
At closing time
The bar-keep rousts them out
In the frigid night they slump
Perhaps dreaming of friends they did not find
In the frigid Alaskan night they slump and sleep,
Forever.

ELDER'S SONG OF LOOKING BACKWARD: TIGARA, ALASKA 1967

Now that I go toward the end of my days in this place
I find joy in looking backward
And I give thanks for this joy.
As a small boy
When the sun crept up
Sending white light through the small square of white man's glass
I watched the beams glide gently across the floor
Encouraging the dust motes to whirl and dance
And I felt joy
And when the moon came, raising her round face before the open summer door
Hugging the horizon before starting her nightly journey
I watched the stars greet her with little glimmers
And I felt joy
When I could not sleep at night when old age kept me awake
I found joy in looking backwards
How glorious was my life in winter
Cold winds and snow even they brought me joy
I scattered my worries into the long night
And I felt joy
I was ever anxious for the summer days to come
I tried to hurry them into being
I hunted and I feasted
And I felt joy
Now that I go toward the end of my days in this place
I find joy in looking backward
Life!
Was it so beautiful?
It was, it was.
When I found the woman to be my wife
When my child came
When I found honors in the feasting house
When I gave to others
When my granddaughter was born
I felt joy
I find joy in looking backward
I tell you this now, life was good to me on this earth
And I feel joy
Joy fills my life
And when the next daylight breaks
And the sun creeps in to encourage the dust motes to dance in his beams
I will again give thanks for this joy
This great joy called life.

ORIGINS; MYTHS OF THE ARCTIC RIM

When the world was in darkness
In the beginning
There was only a small bit of land
No bigger than the house
That sat on this bit of land
In the house lived an old man and his daughter
She collected snow
To melt
For drinking water
One day she knelt to scrape up snow
A feather blew toward her on the wind
She opened her mouth
In surprise
The feather blew in
She swallowed it
She was then pregnant
And the baby she birthed
Was strange
A raven's beak where a mouth should be
The child was a joy
But curious and difficult to tend
One day Raven-Child
Spied a bladder up near the smoke hole
He fussed to play with it
Played a while then broke it
And the sunlight inside the bladder
Leaked out into the world
But the old man
Snatched the bladder from the child
Sealed it
Thus we have both day and night
Another time
Raven stole his grandfather's kayak
Paddled out to sea
Saw a great mound of earth bobbing in the sea
Thought it a whale
Harpooned the land
Towed it to this place and fixed it here
Solid and permanent
So it is because of Raven
People have been able to live
On this land, this world ever since.

THE RITUAL OF SURVIVAL; GREENLAND, 1869

All animals can talk
All have the ability to reason
They are like men
They think, they feel, they react
They observe us men
They know who is clever
Who is slothful or incompetent
These things
they cannot abide
Animals will not come to lazy men
They do not come to just anyone
nor do they favor the most skillful
of hunters, it is not chance or luck
It is the ritual of survival we must employ
Animals need to be wooed
won over
enticed
with cajolery and magic songs
We men bow before the animals
Beg them
Plead with them
Plead for them to come to our lances
our traps and nets
We must suspend our pride to beg so
And fawning before them we plead
We do not like to be so humbled
before the animals
but we do it
for our lives depend upon
the animals
The animals we entice
with begging
charms and magic songs
Our rituals of survival

FOOD FOR MY CHILDREN: MAKENZIE RIVER AREA, CANADA 1960

the split hooves click
the split hooves clack
caribou stream past me
past my hiding spot
in the mass of willows
at the edge of the wide river
the river marsh is icy
on my belly I crawl
wet and shivering
I crawl to the grazing herd
slowly I wiggle along
wet and soaking
I crawl unseen
to be with in range
of the feeding herd
nibbling damp moss
all unexpected I rise
stand feet apart
among the willows
of the icy marsh
the caribou scatter
in headlong flight
one bull one young bull
stops stares at me in surprise
I draw back the bowstring
sighting carefully
along my arm
my aim is sure
my arm is steady
my arrow sings
speeding on its path
my arrow stands quivering
deep in the chest of the bull
I have made
food for my children
here at the edge of the wide river
among the massed willows
in the icy marsh

THE WAYS OF THE LITTLE PEOPLE: KIVALINA, ALASKA 1952

You must never doubt
The dwarves
The little people
Still exist
Out there in homes
But we do not know where
No one has found their homes
Beneath the earth
where
They live

Only as high as your knee
They dress like men
Speak the language of men
Very well
And sing
They have fine voices
But beware
They are both
Capricious and hostile

You can never catch them
All their tracks
All the trails
Eventually lead to the sea
If you hurl a stone
They disappear
If you chase them
They vanish

The little men
The dwarves
The little people
Have great appetites
If you leave a whale on the beach
They will devour it overnight
Try to prevent their thievery
Or reclaim your whale
And the little men
Will cause
Lumps to grow on your body
And your face to swell

NORTHERN LIGHTS: KOTZEBUE, ALASKA, 1953

Look!
The colours dance across the frozen sky!
Flashing high in the winter night.
Look!
The colours wave and dip, curl and rise.
Look!
The spirits of our people
Are playing a game.
The spirits of our people
Are leaping, running, playing ball.
The spirit ones play a game of kickball
With a walrus head
Thrown around
Up there in the sky.
The spirits run, kick
And leap
Playing a game.
And lighting up the winter sky.

SHELIKOF STRAIGHT: GULF OF ASLASKA, 1977

Out there in the water
The icy water of the Straight
Named for a Russian voyager
Now long dead
His name floats on the water
Shelikof Shelikof Shelikof
The waves whisper his name against the rocky shore
When they are not angry
Sometimes the wind shreds the waves
Steals their whispering voices
Turns their murmurs into foam
Tosses it high
Plays with the foam
Like a fox with a feather
Then the winds,
Howling and shrieking
Rush out to sea
Driving waves and foam ahead
And calm returns briefly
Then the silver swimmers come
In the bay, Uyak Bay
beneath the shelter
of lush mountains
the salmon gather
pink salmon with gleaming skins
Silver hordes, anxious
To go up rivers
They parallel the shore, each
Searching for one special river
The river where they were born
The silver swimmers
Are going home
To spawn and die
They jostle in the water
They jump
They flash like mirrors
Even in this grey weather
This overcast
Of Uyak Bay
On Shelikof Straight

COLOURS OF MY WORLD: KIANA, ALASKA 1954

Awake
I am awake
I rise
I rise from sleep
Grey sleep
I stand
I stand on two feet
I greet the day
White day
I look
I look around
I look at raven
Black Grandfather
I see
I see the sky
I reach for the sky
Grey sky
My world
My world needs colour
I see only white and black
Black and white
And
Too much grey
grey
grey

LONLINESS: POINT BARROW, ALASKA 1953

Sometimes
Even when people throng
I feel loneliness
Sometimes when the people act joyous
I feel loneliness
Sometimes when the people dance the songs
I feel loneliness
My Grandfather says I am sister to the loon
This is the source of my loneliness

THE WOMAN WHO ATE HER HUSBAND: ARSUK, GREENLAND 1899

To see her
eyes, red and sunken
into dark circled caverns in a face
stretched drum-tight on her skull
skeletal! bones protruded
her arms deer-leg thin
the voice soft
muttering words
not quite human
the muttered words
cracked parched and thin
she broke down between words
trying to say this:

> I am not one fit to live among my fellows
> Not one who can live among the people
> For I have eaten the flesh of my dearest of kin
> An eater of men, that is what I have become.

her hovel
a dome of snow blocks
one piece of skin
frayed and worn
was her rug and bed
half hidden in a drift, she lived or tried to live
beside this crude dwelling
a human skull
and bones, the flesh gnawed from them
she turned to us
eyes bloodshot with weeping
for the suffering she endured
the cracked words continued
words came between sobs

> Forgive me! Forgive me, my rescuers
> Do not condemn me
> I have done that to myself
> I have eaten my husband and children
> I ate my clothing and all that I could

we lifted her up
to carry her back home
she was but bones and dry skin, seemed empty of blood
we looked at this living skeleton once a young woman.
my companion wept, for he knew her
and this is what he said.

> No one will blame you; none will condemn
> You had the will to live, therefore you live.

WHEN I WAS YOUNG: KING ISLAND, ALASKA 1939

When I was young
O, when I was young
Each new day was a beginning
The beginning of some new thing
When I was young
O, when I was young
Every evening ended
Ended with a promise
Promised me the glow
Of the next day's new dawn
When I was young
O, when I was young

A LITTLE SISTER'S SONG FOR A BABY BROTHER; POINT BARROW, ALASKA 1957

Hush
Hush my little one
Do not weep, little brother
Our mother is coming
Coming soon to fetch us
She has gone to catch cod
Sweet cod for you
Hush
Hush my little one
Do not weep, little brother
Our mother is coming for you
As soon as she fills her basket
Full to the top
Fat cod for you
Hush little brother
Be patient like me

A CHANT TO DISPELL THE COLD: KOTZEBUE, ALASKA 1958

Cold! Cold!
You can not touch me.
See, I stamp my feet
Frost! Frost!
You cannot harm me.
See I wave my arms
I stomp and wave
And
wave and stomp
to drive away the cold and frost!
Cold! Cold!
Frost! Frost!
Away! Away!

SEDNA'S HUSBAND: BAFFIN ISLAND, CANADA 1868

Your ugly body
Your hairless dog-body
Your giant size your fearful eyes
They do not frighten me
Dog-Husband of Sedna
Sedna who rules the sea
Command your husband
He who guards your underwater world
Command him to keep away from me
And stay beneath the sea.
He guards the dead in your sea kingdom
And will not let the living in
I live still
So send him to another place and not to this house
For if he comes
I will rise from this bed of sickness
Beat your dog-husband
And
harness him to my sled!

WHITE NIGHT, WHITE SIREN, WHITE DEATH:
ANAKTUVUK PASS, 1958

A caribou hunter
Alone, stalks the prey
Two cows and a young bull
Have left their tracks
Heading for the river's edge
A caribou hunter
Alone, follows the trail on pack-snow
The air is solid with cold
The night-wind dies
He reaches the roiling river's edge
A caribou hunter
Alone, hears a voice
A lovely voice, a woman singing

> *Come! Come to me!*
> *Hunter all alone*
> *Come lie with me in the night's stillness.*

A caribou hunter
Alone, ran after the voice
Followed the song, a man possessed.
Along the bank he ran.

> *Come! Come to me!*
> *Hunter all alone*
> *Come lie with me in the night's stillness*

A caribou hunter
Alone, saw the woman
A lovely young woman
Beckoning from the opposite shore
He hesitates before the icy river
She sings again

> *Come! Come to me!*
> *Hunter all alone*
> *Come share my bed come share my delights*

A caribou hunter
Alone, throws off his clothes
Battles the icy current
Half dead he reaches the other side
And staggers to approach her
The young beauty scornfully laughs
Becomes a white owl and flys away

With mocking hooting
Alone, half dead
The man swims back
falls prostrate to the ground
His chilled brain flutters
And then it fades
Unconcious and naked
On the shore he freezes
And here
His comrades found him
But none could understand
The sight of
A caribou hunter
Alone, frozen
his warm clothing at his side
All thought he'd lost his senses
his reason had fled they said
If only he could speak of the quarry he hunted
white wings, white siren, white death.

SONG OF THE OLD MAN: KING ISLAND, ALASKA 1939

When I sit here
Beside this old one
This old woman who is my wife
I sometimes
By chance
Think of my childhood
Live again in my youth
All of my memories
Alive as in old days
When all meat was juicy
No quarry too swift for my feet
No woman who could not be won
Now
I have only the old stories and songs
And this old woman who sits at my side

SONG OF THE YOUNG MAN: KING ISLAND, ALASKA 1939

When I sit here
Beside this young one
This beauty who is my wife
I sometimes
By chance
Think of my future
Try to envision the rest of my life
I want to live to see children
I might die on the ice
I wish to earn honors and praise
In the house of the men
I hope my grandchildren bless me
I would like to live to be old
Now
I have only today and few yesterdays
And this beautiful woman who sits at my side

INUIT, I AM: REPULSE BAY, CANADA 1920

Inuit, I am
One of the true people
The real people
The Inuit
The real men
I am strong in the chest
I breathe the cold with out fear.
My legs are short,
Better for the travelling far
My feet are flat
Wide like the snowshoe hare
Better for walking
My arms are strong
Better for hauling oogruk and seal
My teeth are sharp
Better for eating frozen flesh
I walk with strong muscles
Like sinews of Caribou
I pull with strong arms
with the strength of the walrus
Like the great bear, Nannuk,
I fear not the cold
Inuit, I am
A real person

WHAT I LIKE TO SEE: AKALAVIK, CANADA 1956

What I like to see
Caribou
Flocking down from the forests
Starting to travel, wandering north
Grazing and trotting, bellowing bulls
What I like to see
Caribou
Rivers of hoofed ones
The black toes clicking and clacking
Great herds from the forest
Flooding out over the white plains
What I like to see
Caribou
Seeking a crossing place
Searching the river banks for that spot
That's what I like to see.

HOMELAND: ALASKA 2003

Your eight stars of gold
In that midnight blue
Are draped around my heart
That banner is etched on my soul
Your mountains
White, thrusting, unbelievable
Your tundra-plain, wet-footed spruce
The long cold winter nights
Frost-festooned trees reflecting the flares and curtains
Of the northern lights
Powder snow on Aleyska's trails
Popping ice on Kenai Lake
Spring breakup with its mud and slush
Nenana's crumbling ice
Southeast's green and greenery with
Your scudding clouds and dripping skies
Your hidden trails
Green-ferned and thick with devils club
The flashing silver in the summer streams
The browsing moose in distant pond
Antlers dripping golden water lilies
The agility of curved-horn hosts
Scampering the slopes of crescent lakes
White beluga
Hunting in the Turnagain Arm
Bore tides thundering in their wake
Bear trails and bike trails
Quiet rural life, in time, a century behind
And the New-York-Hustle-Bustle of the city
The people; The harmony of the people
Worlds apart they meet and mingle
Becoming Alaskans
Quick to be friends
Helping hands always outstretched
So I am enraptured
Forever captured by your grandeur
Forever charmed by your beauty
You and I are inseparable
You have my heart
And when I'm gone; my life here ended,
Perhaps the Creator
Will allow my captured soul to fly North to be with you

About this Book

Songs, stories, legends and chants of the *Eskimo* people of the Arctic Rim and Alaska, the Yupik, Inuit, Inupiat, Chukchi, Inuvialiut, Loucheux, Denendeh and other Northern First Nations make up the material from which these *"word-sketches"* are made. The author prefers not to call this collection 'poetry' but in one way that is what this book is: poetry. Here then is a sort of poetry where stories of life's experiences are distilled into feelings and thoughts that are universal. Tales taken from real-life travels and adventures among the dwellers of the land of the white dawn are in these pages. Here are tales of love, betrayal, courage, defeat, acceptance, loss. grief, passion, delight, courting, coming of age, birth and death, youth and old age, hunting and surviving. The day to day existence; the business of survival in a harsh land is the theme, the people, places and animals of Alaska and the Northland are the subjects. These great people, their lives entwined and dependent upon one another in the inhospitable world they inhabit, inspired me to create these *"word-sketches"* detailing a land, its people and animals, at many points in time and in many places across the Arctic Rim.

About the Author

Jacques L. Condor (Maka Tai Meh) was a resident of over fifty years in Alaska and the Pacific Northwest Coast. Condor has lived in Japan, Borneo, the Philippines, Canada and Argentina. He has taught the art, history and culture of his Native American Algonkin Heritage as he traveled. In the states he has been an instructor for the Federal Government's Indian Education Program, (Title IV, V, IX) and taught in Iowa, California, Alaska, Colorado, Washington, Oregon and Arizona. He has traveled extensively in Alaska and Canada among the first Nations peoples collecting legends, songs, dances and stories. Among Condor's books is a collection of Native American stories of suspense and fantasy based upon some of these legends; published in 2001 under the title: *CONDOR TALES*.

Condor has had a varied career as a college professor, art director, gallery owner, TV and stage actor and director, film actor and children's art and drama teacher. He has been the recipient of two state arts grants to research Alaska Native music and stories and three grants from the state of California to develop Native American Theatre. Retiring in 1999, he began to devote his time to writing.

Jacques L. Condor, who is now 75, lives with his wife, Diana Seno, in Sun City, Arizona. He devotes his time to writing, painting and his granddaughter, Madeline.

He has four more books forthcoming: another poetry anthology, *CHILDREN OF THE TURTLE, Native American Poetry, AN ALASKAN TRILOGY OF TER-ROR: The Blood Drinker of Cooper Landing, The girls of Potter Marsh, The Thing in Skilak Lake* and two books of Native American stories for children.

Suggested Reading

1. ACROSS ARCTIC AMERICA, a narrative of the fifth Tule expedition by Knud Rasmussen, G.P. Putman & Sons, 1927

2. AGAGUK, by Yves Theriault, Tyerson Press, Toronto, 1963

3. ALASKA, by Bern Keating, National Geographic Society, 1969

4. ALASKA BIRD TRAILS, by Herbert Brandt, Bird Research Foundation, 1943

5. ALASKA'S NATIVE PEOPLE, by Lael Morgan, Vol. 16 No. 3, Alaska Geographic Society, Anchorage,

6. ALASKAN ADVENTURES, by Loyal L. Wirt, Fleming H. Revel & Co., London 1937

7. ALASKAN ESKIMO CEREMONIALISM, by Margaret Lantis, Univ. of Washington, 1966

8. ALASKA, THE LAST FRONTIER, by Bryan Cooper, William Morrow, 1973

9. A LEGACY OF ARCTIC ART, by Dorothy Jean Ray, Univ. of Washington, 1996

10. ALEXANDER MACKENZIE, CANADIAN EXPLORER, by Ronald Syme, William Morrow, 1962

11. ANERKA, by Edmund Carpenter and Enooeseweetok, J. M. Dent & Sons, Toronto, 1959

12. ANCIENT CULTURES OF THE BERING SEA AND THE ESKIMO, by Sergi Rudenko, University of Toronto Press, 1961

13. THE ARCTIC YEAR, Freuchen and Salomonsen, G.P. Putman & Sons, 1958

14. THE ARCTIC PRARIES, by Ernest Thompson Seton, International Univ. Press, 1943

15. ARCTIC WILD, by Lois Crisler, Harper & Row, Publishers, 1956

16. ARCTIC WORLD, by Marco Nazarri, White Star Publishers, 1990

17. APOSTLE OF THE ICE AND SNOW by Eva B. Betz, Theo Gaus & Sons, 1960

18. AYORAMA, by Raymond de Coccola & Paul King, Oxford Univ. Press 1956

19. BOOK OF ESKIMOS, BY Peter Freuchen, Brambell House, Publishers 1961

20. BEYOND THE HIGH HILLS, by Guy Mary-Rousseliere, World Publishing, 1961

21. BIRDS OF ALASKA, by Ira N. Gabrielson & Frederick C. Lincoln, The Stackpole Co., 1959

22. BIRD GIRL, by Velma Wallis, Epicenter Press, Canada, 1996

23. CANADA, EXPLORING FROM SEA TO SEA, by Robert L. Breeden, National Geographic Society, 1971

24. CHILDREN OF THE MIDNIGHT SUN, BY Tricia Brown and Roy Corral, Alaska-Northwest books, 2001

25. COLD STARRY NIGHT, by Claire Fejes, Epicenter Press, 1996

26. DANCE ON A SEALSKIN, by Barbara Winslow and Terri Sloat, Alaska-Northwest Books, 1996

27. DAWN IN ARCTIC ALASKA, by Diamond Jenness, Univ. of Minnesota, 1957

28. DRUMS OF DIOMEDE, by Arthur Hansen Eide, House Warven Publishers, 1952

29. ESKIMOS, by Kaj Birkit-Smith, Methuen & Co. Publishers, 1959

30. ESKIMOS, by Wally Herbert, Collins Publishers, Glasgow, 1977

31. ESKIMO ART, by Cottie Burland, The Hamlin Company, London, 1973

32. ESKIMO LIFE, by Robert Mayokok, Nome Nugget Press, 1965

33. ESKIMO MASKS, ART AND CEREMONY, by Dorothy Jean Ray, Univ. Washington, 1967

34 FIFTY YEARS IN ALASKA, by Carl G. Lomen, Van Rees Press, 1954

35 FOUR SEASONS NORTH, by Billie Wright, Harper & Row, 1973

36 HUNTERS OF THE NORTHERN FOREST, by Richard K. Nelson, Univ. of Chicago, 1986

37. I AM ESKIMO; AKNIK MY NAME, by Paul Green, Alaska-Northwest, 1959

38. IGLOO TALES, by Edward L. Keithahn, United Indian Services Publication, 1953

39. IPIUTAK AND THE ARCTIC WHALE HUNTING CULTURE, by Helge Larsen and Froelich Rainey, American Museum of natural History, 1948

40. KABLOONA, by Gontran de Poncins, Reynal and Hitchcock, New York, 1941

41. LAST NEW LAND, edited by Wayne Mergler, Alaska-Northwest Books, 1996

42. MAKE PRAYERS TO THE RAVEN, by Richard K. Nelson, Univ. of Chicago, 1983

43. NATURALIST IN ALASKA, by Adolph Murie, the Devin-Adair Co., 1961
NUNAGA, by Duncan Pryde, Walker & Company, 1971

44. ON THE EDGE OF NOWHERE, by James Huntington, Crown Publishers, 1966

45. PEOPLE OF THE NOATAK, by Claire Fejes, Volcano Press, California, 1998

46. PEOPLE OF THE TWILIGHT, by Diamond Jenness, Univ. of Chicago, 1959

47. POINT HOPE, AN ESKIMO VILLAGE IN TRANSITION, by James W. VanStone, Univ. of Washington, 1962

48. TWO OLD WOMEN, by Velma Wallis, Harper-Collins, NY, 1994

49. ROOTS OF TICASUK, by Emily Ivanoff Brown, Alaska-Northwest Publishing, 1982

50. SHADOW OF THE HUNTER, by Richard K. Nelson, Univ. of Chicago, 1983

51. TALES OF TICASUK, by Emily Ivanoff Brown, Univ. of Alaska Press, 1995

52. THE GIRL WHO DREAMED ONLY OF GEESE, by Howard Norman, Gulliver Books, Harcourt-Brace & Co., 1997

53. THE CENTRAL ESKIMO, by Franz Boaz, Univ. of Nebraska Press, 1967

54. THE GHOST OF KINGIKTY, by Lela Kiana Oman, Ken Wray Printers, Anchorage, 1967

55. THE ESKIMO OF NORTH AMERICA, by Norman A. Chance, Holt-Reinhardt & Winston, 1966

56. THE LYNX POINT PEOPLE, by June Helm, National Museum of Canada, 1961

57. THE VILLAGE PEOPLE, by Staff Writers of the Anchorage Daily News, 1966

58. TWO IN THE FAR NORTH, by Margaret E. Murie, Alfred A.Knopf, 1962

59. UGIUVANGMIUT QULIAPYUIT, King Island Tales, compiled by Lawrence D. Kaplan and Margret Yocom, Univ. of Alaska Press, 1988

60. WHITE DAWN, James Houston, Harcourt-Brace & Jovanovich, Inc., 1971

61. WILD ALASKA, by American Wilderness Time-Life Books, 1973

62. WILD VOICES OF THE NORTH, by Sally Carrighar, Doubleday & Co., 1959 and
MOONLIGHT AT MIDDAY
ICEBOUND SUMMER

0-595-28867-7

CPSIA information can be obtained at www.ICGtesting.com
Printed in the USA
235825LV00004B/140/A

9 780595 288670